SIMMONDS ON BANK INSURANCE

2ND EDITION

INSURANCE ADVICE FOR COMMUNITY BANKERS

SCOTT SIMMONDS

Scott Simmonds, CPCU, ARM
Insurance from an Unbiased Point of View
(207) 284-0085
Scott@ScottSimmonds.com
www.ScottSimmonds.com

Bank Resource Center – www.BankInsuranceConsultant.com
Published by Insurance Consultants of Maine, Inc.
Published in the United States
by Insurance Consultants of Maine, Inc.,
Saco, Maine
First Edition ISBN: 0-9774015-2-9
Second Edition ISBN: 1466235284
Second Edition ISBN 13: 9781466235281
Printed in the United States of America

Contents

NOTE: The use of a ★ in the text indicates that a section is either new or significantly updated since the first edition of this book.

Introduction

For almost thirty years now, I have been helping banks with their insurance. In the first two-thirds of that time, I was an insurance agent, selling insurance.

Since 2000, I have been an insurance consultant. I work for insurance buyers, helping them buy and manage their insurance. I never sell insurance and never accept fees or commissions from the insurance agents I work with for my clients.

This book is written for community bankers who buy insurance for their banks.

Most banks work with a local insurance agent, often someone with a direct connection to the board. I have worked with bankers whose agents are board members or stockholders. Sometimes it's the agent's father who is/was on the board. I have worked with banks where the president's wife's brother is the agent. Some of my bank clients own their insurance agents.

Often, a bank's agent handles the insurance for only one bank. That is no way to really understand an industry and the risk/insurance issues of the industry. That's why I am brought in to help.

In 2005, I started thinking about a book about bank insurance issues. The first edition of this book was published in 2007. Since then, much has changed in the worlds of banking and bank insurance. There are hundreds of changes in this, the second edition.

I believe that the mathematical formula for calculating insurance change is the insured's industry change squared, times the insurance industry change, cubed. (Wink.)

In this edition, I have added almost a hundred sections, definitions, and ideas. I have tuned some of the work gently in some places, and in other places, the changes in my recommendations are wholesale. I read some of the stuff I wrote in 2007 and cringed. The ideas, however, were right at the time.

I hope you find this volume helpful and informative. Your questions and comments are welcome. I will incorporate them into the third edition.

All the tools and documents mentioned in this book can be found at www.ScottSimmonds.com/bankbook2 in word processor format for ease of use.

Scott Simmonds, CPCU, ARM
Saco, Maine
February, 2014

Chapter One: General Insurance Issues

Your Agent Is a VIP (Vital Insurance Partner)

My friend Howard Candage taught me that the most important part of the insurance transaction is the relationship an insurance buyer has with his or her insurance agent. Having the right agent is critical to a successful insurance program. There has to be trust and respect between the two parties.

Your relationship with your agent has to be as trusting as the relationship you have with your lawyer or accountant.

Insurance agents can be either employees of the insurance company for whom they sell (called direct writers) or independent business people who work for themselves. Independent agents usually represent more than one insurance company. While each will tell you that his or her approach is best, I find that both independent agents and direct writers have a place in the market.

1

Most community banks do business with independent agents. Often it's an agent from the community. No two agencies have the same abilities or resources. No two agents have the same level of knowledge and expertise.

When the chips are down, your agent can make all the difference in a claim or coverage dispute. Make sure that your agent can meet your needs. Here are some questions as you review an agent's services:

- Who will manage your account on a daily basis?

- How long have the producer and service people been in the insurance business?

- Will the agent provide advice on all aspects of bank insurance?

- Does the agency have special expertise in banks and financial institutions?

- How are claims handled? Does the agency have a claims department?

- Will one person in the agency oversee claim incident reports?

- Who will provide help preventing losses—the agent, the insurer, or both?

It is common for banks to buy insurance from an agent who is a customer of the bank. Many banks use several agents to "spread the wealth." I've worked with banks where one agent handles the property insurance, another handles auto insurance, and still another handles directors' and officers' insurance. Consider this strategy carefully. You may be opening yourself up to misunderstandings in terms of exposure and coverage. In such a setup, one agent may not know what coverage the other agents are providing. If you are going to work with multiple agents, consider building a list of coverages showing all policies. Share the list with all your agents so each knows what the others are doing.

My recommendation is usually that a business should have one insurance agent handle all the property and casualty insurance needs.

Insurance is Not Gambling

Countless people over the years have told me that buying insurance is nothing more than gambling. Not true. Gambling creates risk, while insurance addresses and protects you from existing risk. When you gamble, you can finish in one of three places: as a winner, as a loser, or as someone who has broke even. You can also choose not to play.

Insurance addresses the risks you already face. You own a building. You must be sure it's still there tomorrow. The next day, the building either is there or is not. Insurance, unlike gambling, does not create risk.

Insurance passes the risk of loss from you to the insurance company. That's why "self-insurance" is a misnomer. You either buy insurance or you don't. If you don't buy insurance, you are funding the risk yourself, which is also known as "retention;" you retain the risk.

Be an Exceptional Risk

Obtaining favorable insurance rates depends in part on you. Maintain your buildings. Insist on safe work habits. Train your employees to manage emergencies.

Put your best foot forward with your insurance company (current or potential) when inspectors show up. Housekeeping is important when insurers are evaluating your operation. Go on a pre-inspection walk-through, looking at your operations, branches, and locations as an insurance company would. Make sure fire extinguishers are up-to-date and properly located. Electric panels and appliances should be installed correctly. Extension cords should be removed or replaced by hardwired outlets. Pick up trash and clean up storage rooms.

Show insurers that you're a quality risk by having policies and procedures in place to control losses and manage claims.

Good Maintenance = Premium Credits

One bank client learned the hard way that housekeeping is important.

Three months prior to the bank's insurance renewal, the insurer inspected the branch offices. I told the CFO that the bank's maintenance team should do a thorough, pre-inspection walk-through to prevent any surprises. I gave him a rundown of the things the inspector would be looking for, including fire extinguishers, use of extension cords, fire safety issues, general housekeeping, electrical code violations, and a review of any cooking exposures or potential for loss in employee break areas.

Several weeks later, I received a call from the bank's agent telling me that the underwriter had removed most of the premium credits for the upcoming package policy renewal. Apparently, the inspection had not gone well.

I urged the agent to get a copy of the deficiencies and ask the underwriter for an agreement that if all deficiencies were remedied within three weeks, the credits would be returned to the policy. The resulting premium credit to the policy was a savings of 15 percent to the bank.

Loss Prevention Is Always Your Best Tactic

What can you do to prevent accidents and losses? How can you make your operation safer?

It is always less expensive to prevent a loss than to have one. Inspect your properties regularly and look for problems. How would an insurance company inspector view your offices? What can be done to make the property safer and less prone to an accident or loss?

Consider ways to control the losses that do occur. Sprinkler systems minimize the damage caused by a fire. Expand your video surveillance system to show your parking lots. Having a clean desk policy in your administration center can limit the losses if the sprinkler or plumbing system fails. Exceptional data backup procedures limit downtime.

Look for practical ways to limit and prevent losses.

Consider Your Renewal Dates Carefully

The most popular renewal date for business insurance programs is January 1. July 1 is also common. The "quarter changes" of April and October are busy times for insurance companies too.

Don't renew your insurance anywhere near these dates. Underwriters and agents are scurrying around trying to handle three or four times their normal workload. Unless you are spending $1 million a year on your insurance, you won't get the attention you deserve. If you currently have one of the above policy dates, consider changing it to a date like February 17 or June 12.

One exception: Rarely do I recommend changing policy dates on workers' compensation policies. The experience modification calculation does not respond well to changing policy periods. See the section of this report on workers' compensation for more information.

Renewals – Use Competition in an Intelligent Way

Competition with renewal is not one agent quoting your policies with three insurers. Competition puts your agent and insurers in jeopardy of losing your business if they don't sharpen their pencils. It is only natural that an agent will work harder when there is the threat of losing you as a client.

Be cautious, however. Most insurers only provide quotes to one agent in a bid. It's called market blocking—insurers accept the first application submitted. No other agents can quote that insurer.

Having two agents attempting to access the same insurer creates conflict and infighting between the agents, which will hamper your bid efforts. Be sure the competing agents bring insurers into the bid process that your current agent can't access. Consider national specialty programs to compete with your local agent. This adds a different flavor to the bid process. Direct writers such as Liberty Mutual can help too.

An integral part of the bid process is your control over which agent uses which insurance company. More information on this topic can be found in chapter twenty-five.

A Downside to Bidding

Above I've outlined the conflict that can occur when two agents access the same insurer. Assigning insurers to specific agents can also lead to imperfect combinations of coverage.

The best insurance program does not always come from one insurance company. Perhaps Company A has the best auto program, while Company B has the best package policy. If you assign Company A to Agent A and Company B to Agent B, you will not be able to use one agent for the all-around best insurance program. You could cherry-pick. However, using two agents comes with its own set of troubles.

For more information on the bid process, see chapters eighteen through twenty-one.

Consider Competition Without Bidding

The best approach to getting the best insurance program may not be the traditional bid process. A broker selection process allowing presentations from several agents can work well. Each broker outlines his or her approach and services. Sometimes the best approach is a conceptual proposal that includes a broker's suggestions on coverage and service improvements.

Build a list of agents that you think can provide the service and expertise you require. Get names from colleagues and other bankers. Prepare a summary of your current insurance, including insurers and premiums, along with a detailed description of your business. Prepare a questionnaire that agents can complete. Ask about services provided, résumés of the people who will handle the account, and insurers who will work with you.

See appendix two for forms to help with the broker selection process.

What if You Can't Change Agents?

About 60 percent of the community banks I work with cannot—or will not—change insurance agents. Perhaps your agent is a stockholder. Maybe you own your insurance agency. I have several clients who have strong marketing agreements with their agent. Sometimes the agent is the best friend (or brother-in-law) of either the owner of the bank or the CEO.

Get outside help. I realize this may sound self-serving, as I do make my living providing these consulting services. However, without another competing agent or consultant reviewing the work of your agent, you will have no idea if you have the right insurance or not.

Another option is my bank insurance toolbox (www.InsuranceBookShop.com), which provides pages and pages of questions you can ask your agent to start a conversation about insurance coverage.

Review Coverage for Value

Review all your insurance coverage to determine the true value in light of current premium levels. Many banks have added earthquake, flood, and machinery breakdown coverage in years past. Is the coverage worth the current premium? Are your premium dollars better spent in other areas? Is the cost of the coverage worth the value of the protection? Consider catastrophic losses as you review your insurance for value.

All decisions are value decisions. Unfortunately, sometimes insurance coverage is considered a basket where you only add items—never reducing what you buy. Sometimes it makes sense to pare back.

Reducing Insurance Coverage

Insurance agents hate to reduce coverage, and it isn't just the idea of losing commissions that is abhorrent to them. Almost every trade magazine your insurance agent reads has horror stories about insurance agents getting sued for claim problems. Insurance agents get it drummed into their heads that their clients are out to sue them. Most agents attend educational events where the speakers talk about "E&O Nightmares." (Errors and omissions, the professional liability insurance that agents buy.)

Listen to the recording your agent has on his or her voicemail. Read the disclaimer your agent puts at the end of his or her emails. Most agents are absolutely paranoid about this stuff.

Go ahead and consider reducing your insurance. Nothing sacred here! Just because you have a $12 million umbrella policy this year does not mean you have to buy that same limit next year. Having the peril of earthquake on your policy now might make sense. Next year, the premium for quake may be too high. My advice might be to remove the coverage. Your agent will probably make you sign a letter and swear a blood oath to reduce any part of your coverage.

If it makes economic sense, buy more coverage. If not, buy less.

Start the Policy Renewal Process Early

You'll need at least 120 days to "work" the renewal of your insurance program. If you're getting quotes from other agents, it will take time to develop bid specs and gather the information and data that the underwriters will need.

Even if you're not bidding, talk with your insurance agent early in the process. He or she should know what your current insurer is planning. Ask about premiums and coverage. Many carriers add exclusions and restrictions to renewal policies. Get at least a ballpark renewal quote as early as possible. Push your agent and insurer. You're the customer!

If you are not bidding your insurance, insist on getting renewal indications at least ninety days before your insurance expires.

See Chapter Twenty-Two for more info on the renewal process.

Review Your Insurer's Financial Ratings

Every year, insurance companies go out of business. In the past twenty years, more than six hundred insurers became insolvent, severely impacting their clients. Claims went unpaid. Policies had to be replaced quickly, resulting in lower coverage and higher premiums—not a fun time.

Several organizations analyze the soundness of insurance companies. The best known is the AM Best Company (www.ambest.com). Standard & Poor's also rates insurers. I rely on Weiss Ratings (www.WeissRatings.com) as a tough, unbiased source of information. They never accept fees from insurers. They utilize industry and regulator filings in their analyses. They're tough graders, too; a B- is still considered good in their system.

A recent review of AM Best Ratings revealed that almost 90 percent of insurance companies receive a rating of "Very Good" or better. Only 29 percent of insurers received a Weiss Rating of "Good" or better. I believe that Weiss has a higher standard. When working with my clients' money, I want objective, tough, and accurate ratings.

An insolvent insurer means your coverage is compromised. Use rating organizations such as AM Best and Weiss Ratings to help you make informed decisions.

Remember the Pollution Exclusion

Over the past twenty years, the insurance industry has been hammered by the courts on pollution claims. Now, most standard insurance policies have pollution exclusions so broad that the industry calls them "absolute pollution exclusions."

Liability arising out of pollution is excluded by most general liability insurance policies. If the oil tank for your heating system leaks and pollutes your neighbor's well, there is no coverage.

Directors' and officers' policies also have pollution exclusions.

Your property insurance is also likely to have an exclusion for damage to your property caused by pollution—either your pollution or pollution caused by others.

The only exception to the above is for the cleanup of pollution on your premises caused by a peril included in your property insurance. Coverage is usually limited to $25K.

Pollution Cleanup Expense Example

In most insurance policies, the only pollution coverage is for the cleanup of a spill caused by an insured event at your premises.

Example event: Ice from your roof falls and severs the fuel line of an outside oil tank that runs to your heating system. One hundred and fifty gallons of heating oil spill onto the ground.

In every state, the Environmental Protection Agency requires that the contaminated soil is removed and trucked to a special landfill. Monitoring is mandated, and the hole must be left open for three months to assure complete removal of contaminants. The total cost is usually around $20K.

Learn to Read Your Insurance Policies

The mere thought of reading an insurance policy can make your head hurt. Here are some hints to make it less painful.

Understand the Purpose of the Policy – An auto policy is designed to cover vehicular accidents. General liability insurance is purchased to protect the insured from liability arising out of bodily injury, property damage, personal injury, and advertising injury. Directors' and officers' insurance indemnifies the key people for errors in judgment and bad decisions. Reading a policy with the intent of coverage in mind goes a long way to helping you understand the contract.

Read the Declarations Page – The declarations page is usually the first few pages of the policy. It will contain information specific to the policy being reviewed, such as policy effective and cancellation dates, names of insured, the subject of the insurance policy (list of vehicles, buildings, description of property, etc.), premiums charged, policy form numbers, and form edition dates.

Review the Definitions – In most insurance policies, words that are defined by the policy are in bold type or quotation marks. Find the definition section of the policy and browse the terms. Mark the section of the policy with a paper clip. You'll be going back to it time and time again. Read the endorsements. They can change the definitions.

Read the Insuring Agreement – The insuring agreement is usually the first part of the actual policy wording. It will tell you what is covered by the policy. For property insurance, learn what causes of loss (perils) are insured. For a directors' and officers' insurance policy, look at the definition of "wrongful act."

Review the Exclusions – The exclusions tell you what is not covered by the policy. Most policies start with broad insuring agreements and then whittle away at the coverage with the use of exclusions. Broad exclusions are not necessarily bad. For example, a general liability policy will exclude auto accidents. No problem. That's why you buy an auto insurance policy. Look for exceptions to the exclusion, with wording like, "This exclusion does not apply to. ..." For example, the general liability policy excludes watercraft. There is an exception to the exclusion in most policies for watercraft that you do not own and that are less than twenty-six feet in length. (The exception to the exclusion provides non-owned watercraft coverage if the boat is less than twenty-six feet long.)

Review the Endorsements – The endorsements are usually found at the end of the policy. They amend the standard policy language. It is not unusual to have more than ten endorsements to a policy. The title of the endorsement usually gives you a good idea of what is trying to be accomplished with the form. If an endorsement deletes a section of the policy, mark that section in the policy document for future reference.

Review Policy Conditions – The policy conditions will show you the general "rules of the road" for the contract. Issues like cancellation, arbitration, and claims reporting are usually covered in this section.

Read Your Policies With a Pencil – I read insurance policies with a pencil in hand. I mark sections and summarize the contents of a particular clause in two or three words. It helps me find sections later and ensures that I am not wasting time looking at a section that is amended by an exclusion.

Chapter Two: Property Insurance

Property insurance includes coverage on your buildings, the contents of your buildings, and the loss of income that comes from a fire or other insured cause of loss. There can also be coverage for the increased cost of getting back into business quickly.

How is Your Property Valued?

How do you get paid for property you lose? Who comes up with the value?

Valuation can mean several different things:

- real estate value (the price at which you could sell)
- tax assessment value
- replacement cost
- book value (purchase price minus accounting depreciation)
- actual cash value (replacement cost minus usage depreciation)

Two forms of valuation are commonly used in property insurance. The traditional (meaning old-fashioned) valuation is "actual cash value." The term is defined by most policies as replacement cost minus depreciation. In some states, you must also consider market value in the determination of the actual cash value of property.

Actual Cash Value – Building Example

Suppose that a thirty-year-old building would cost $1.5 million to replace. The structure is well-maintained and in no way obsolete. The roof was replaced last year. Plumbing and electrical have been updated recently. A fire destroys the building.

The insurance company adjuster determines that 20 percent depreciation is called for. She issues a check to the insured for $1.5 million less 20 percent, minus the deductible.

Actual Cash Value – Personal Property Example

Suppose that a pipe in the ceiling of a bank branch office bursts, damaging a conference table, chairs, audio-visual equipment, and several computers. The cost to replace the items is $35K.

The insurance company adjuster determines that the equipment was obsolete and the furniture was in poor repair. Based on photographs and interviews, it is determined that 60 percent depreciation is in order. You are offered $14K (40 percent of $35K), less your deductible.

Replacement cost valuation of property uses the actual cost of buying a replacement item or rebuilding the structure. If the building burned to the ground, how much would it cost to rebuild with the current cost of materials and labor?

Generally, you'll want your insurance to be written on a replacement cost basis. The policy maker agrees to pay the full cost of reconstruction without deduction for depreciation.

Carry actual cash value coverage only when you would not replace a building after a fire—a relatively rare plan.

Personal property can also be valued at replacement cost or based on its actual cash value. Again, in most cases, replacement cost is the most desirable valuation.

Buy the Right Amount of Coverage

Most property policies have severe penalties for underinsurance. The amount of coverage you buy depends on the valuation of the property. Most banks need replacement cost coverage, which is insurance designed to pay for the replacement of your property with new materials and the current cost of labor.

Your agent can help you with estimating the replacement cost of your buildings. Determining the value of contents is tougher. Go through your locations room by room and count thousands of dollars in value (e.g., desk and chair, $1K; three file cabinets, $1K; computer and printer, $2K).

Beware of Coinsurance

Coinsurance is a penalty provision found in most property insurance policies for underinsurance. It never helps you. It can only hurt at the time of a loss.

Example – Underinsured Building With Coinsurance

Property value: $1 million
80 percent coinsurance clause (requires the purchase of $800K of insurance)
Amount of insurance: $750K
Amount of fire loss: $75K
Loss = what you bought, divided by what you should have bought, times the amount of the loss.
Claim payment = $750K divided by $800K = .9375
.9375 multiplied by $75K = $70,313
$75K – $70,313 = $4,687 Coinsurance penalty

Example – Correctly Insured Building with Coinsurance

Property value: $1 million

80 percent coinsurance clause (requires the purchase of $800K of insurance)

Amount of insurance: $850K

Amount of fire loss: $75K

Since the amount of insurance is more than the $800K required by coinsurance, the loss payment is the full $75K (less any deductible).

Most insurers will eliminate the coinsurance clause at your request. Many carriers will add a clause to the policy agreeing that the amount of insurance meets the coinsurance clause—called the agreed amount endorsement. Work with your agent to eliminate any coinsurance clauses from your policies.

Blanket Insurance

Talk with your agent about blanket coverage—one amount of insurance for all your property. Even if your bank is contained in only one building, combining the building and contents insurance into one amount of coverage can help you at the time of a claim.

Example – Specific Insurance

Main building coverage: $1.7 million

Contents of main building: $750K

Elm Street branch building coverage: $750K

Contents of Elm Street branch: $400K

If the Elm Street location burned, the policy would pay up to $750K for the repair of the building and $400K for the replacement of the contents.

Example – Blanket Insurance

Main building coverage: $1.7 million
Contents of main building: $750K
Elm Street branch building coverage: $750K
Contents of Elm Street branch: $400K
Blanket amount of insurance: $3.6 million ($1.7 million + $750K + $750K + $400K)
If the Elm Street location burned, the policy would pay up to $3.6 million for the repair of the building and for the replacement of the contents.

Special Perils

Perils are causes of loss—fire, lightning, wind, or hail, for instance. Policies that include coverage for "special perils" provide the broadest coverage—protection for any cause of loss not excluded by the policy. Common exclusions are earthquake, flood, nuclear events, damage by insects or animals, and mold. If the cause of loss is not excluded by the policy, there is coverage for the damage.

So-called "named peril" policies provide a laundry list of events for which coverage applies—fire, lightning, hail, vehicles, aircraft, windstorm, explosion, and vandalism, for example. If the damage was caused by a peril not listed, there is no coverage.

Put another way, special perils policies cover any cause of loss except what is excluded. Named peril policies cover only causes of loss listed.

"Special perils" is the preferable way for a bank to insure its property.

Machinery Coverage – The Peril of Mechanical Breakdown

Many property insurance policies are now including a new peril that was previously excluded: mechanical breakdown.

Some banks have a "boiler and machinery" policy that provides equivalent coverage. I include a discussion here, as you may find the protection within your property policy.

Consider the events that will cause you to have to replace a phone system, air-conditioning unit, heating system, or another machine or piece of equipment.

Obviously, fire, theft, vandalism, or a windstorm that destroys your building can damage the equipment. All these perils are covered by your property insurance.

How about a voltage surge that blows out the motor of your air conditioning system? How about loss of water in a heating system, causing a crack in the boiler? How about the failure of the lubrication system in an elevator unit, causing overheating and damage to the travel unit?

All of the above are excluded by standard property insurance.

Machinery coverage (a separate policy or an added peril to the property policy) can add protection for the losses described.

Machinery Coverage Comment

In general, banks have little need for machinery coverage. The largest loss I have seen in a bank for machinery or mechanical breakdown is $3,500 for the replacement of some components in an alarm system when a voltage surge hit it. Certainly not a catastrophic loss. Inconvenient? Yes. The bank didn't lose any business though, and the alarm was up and running that afternoon.

I'm not saying banks should ever buy machinery coverage.

If your building is heated with a high-pressure boiler, buy the coverage 100 percent of the time. Otherwise, look at the value of the coverage and your other insurance needs. Is the premium for machinery coverage better spent on additional umbrella liability coverage? Consider using the funds to buy additional limits on your bond or your D&O protection.

What's a Building?

The word "building" should be straightforward, right? Not in the world of insurance!

Most property insurance policies define "building" as a structure including:

- completed additions
- fixtures, including outdoor fixtures
- permanently installed machinery and equipment
- personal property owned by you that is used to maintain or service the building, including fire extinguishing equipment, outdoor furniture, floor coverings, and appliances used for refrigerating, ventilating, cooking, dishwashing, or laundering.

While the policy does not define "fixtures," the term is generally held to entail items such as light poles and flag poles, parking stops, mailboxes, and in-ground sprinkler systems. Signs attached to your building are also considered fixtures. A drive-through awning is a part of the building. The pneumatic tubes at drive-up windows are covered as part of the building. Most insurers would consider an ATM unit to be a fixture—even as a separate kiosk.

ATMs in a separate building should be separately insured and described in most policies.

Under most insurance policies, freestanding signs are covered to $250 or another small amount. Extra coverage can be purchased.

Building additions under construction are covered if you have not purchased other insurance, such as builder's risk. Materials used in the construction of an addition are covered when stored within one hundred feet of the premises.

Consider Buying Flood Insurance

Earlier, I said that flood is excluded from most property insurance policies.

As you consider the peril of flood, don't think of it as water damage. Floodwater is not nice, clean water that happens to be in your lobby. Floods take out septic systems and sewage treatment plants. Dead things will be floating in the basement of your building. Shovels, not mops, are used to clean up the mess. It's dirty, smelly, and disgusting. You'll want help cleaning it up, and insurance can offer that help.

Many insurers will offer flood coverage as part of the package policy. You'll probably have a separate limit. Perhaps the policy will include a limit of $1 million for any location. Is that enough?

Some policies provide flood coverage only to buildings not located in flood zones. Check your policy and talk with your advisor. You may need to buy a separate flood insurance policy.

★ Consider Buying Earthquake Insurance

As I write this, the earthquake of March 2011 in Japan is fresh in my mind. Almost sixteen thousand people lost their lives in a country that is recognized for having one of the most sophisticated warning systems and preparedness plans in the world.

The recent earthquakes that hit Washington, DC, and New York in August 2011 point to the damage that can come from relatively minor shakes.

Intense quakes can hit anywhere. An earthquake hit Boston in 1755 and damaged 1,200 buildings. More than a hundred chimneys were leveled. People on ships in the harbor said they felt like they had run aground because the intensity was so great. Think of what would happen if an earthquake of that same intensity hit Boston now.

Not long ago, I experienced my first earthquake at my home in Maine. My first thought was that the house would collapse. Then I wondered why a train was coming down my street. All the neighbors met in the street within two minutes. One guy thought his furnace had exploded. I guess we are wimps in the Northeast when compared to the residents of California. Ours was a 2.7 quake, and people talked about it for weeks.

Earthquake is excluded under most property insurance policies. Consider adding coverage for this peril.

If you live in quake-prone areas, your agent has undoubtedly discussed the coverage with you. Most agents on the East Coast don't even talk about earthquake with their clients. That might be a mistake.

Talk with your agent. You may be surprised at how inexpensive the coverage is.

Business Interruption and Extra Expense

I am regularly asked to explain business income insurance. First, let's get past semantics. The following terms mean the same thing: business interruption coverage, loss of business income, time element, use, and occupancy. They all describe protection from the loss of income that occurs when a business is shut down due to a fire or other insured loss.

Silly Story to Explain Loss of Business Income Insurance

For many years, I've used the same story to help business owners understand what exactly business income coverage does. It's a silly story, but it makes my point.

Pretend you own a goose (a building). Your goose lays golden eggs (cash flow). If your goose is run over by a truck, it's going to take you nine months to get a new goose (get back into operation). You have insurance that will pay for the cost of the new goose (property insurance), but what about the value of the eggs you won't get in the nine months you're without a goose? Business income coverage pays you the value of the eggs while you're waiting for your new goose.

Part two of business interruption coverage is extra expense—coverage that pays the increased cost of getting your goose in five months instead of waiting nine. It is the most pressing need for business interruption coverage for banks. If a branch is down due to fire or windstorm, the priority is to reopen quickly through a temporary location or bank trailer. Extra expense coverage will pay for the rental.

Insurers will generally provide a blanket limit of extra expense coverage over all locations.

Work with your advisor to determine the correct business income protection for you.

Another point: eliminate coinsurance penalties from business income coverage, if possible.

★ Extra Expense Worksheet

Determining the correct amount of extra expense coverage can be a challenge. Here is a calculation I came up with that can help determine the minimum coverage limit for a specific location. This is alchemy, not science.

Enter The Number of Employees (Full & Part Time) In Box A--->	A	
Multiply A by $5K. Enter in Box B --->	B	
If Computer Center, Put $50K In Box C--->	C	
Per Location Constant	D	$100K
Recommended Minimum Coverage: Total of B+C+D=E --->	E	

The minimum limit of coverage for this location is the value in box E. Consider other issues as well, such as difficulty in getting temporary office space. When in doubt, buy more.

For blanket coverage, buy at least the highest recommended limit multiplied by one-half the total number of locations you have.

Another approach is to have a minimum of $500K on major locations and $250K on minor ones.

If you have an extra expense form that includes coinsurance, buy at least the coinsurance percentage times the total of the recommended minimum coverage. Better yet, get your agent to delete the coinsurance clause.

Deductibles

In my review of bank insurance programs, I find that most banks have relatively low property deductibles. Think of it this way: your home insurance probably has a $500 or $1K deductible, and a few hundred thousand in insurance. Your bank has millions of dollars of insurance. Does a $1K deductible really make sense?

Things happen in our daily lives. Don't use your insurance to pay for the bumps in the road. Look to insurance to help you through catastrophes.

Did vandals damage a sign outside the main office? Why look to insurance to pay for it? Did a windstorm damage a few shingles on the roof of a branch office? Fix them and move on. Insurance should be for when your roof is destroyed, or for a loss that would have a devastating effect on your bank's financial health.

Use high deductibles on your property insurance to reduce your premiums. Consider $5K, $10K, or higher. Small losses are a cost of business. Budget for them.

Note: Never pay liability claims yourself. Report damage to other people's property or injuries to people as soon as possible. Even if it seems that the injury is minor, report the claim to your insurer quickly.

Storage Locations

Review other locations where you may have property, such as warehouses and mini-storage companies. Consider equipment belonging to the bank that is at employees' homes. Telecommuters and executives with bank computers at home may need to be listed on your property insurance policies.

Computer Coverage

Some property insurers segregate computers into a separate limit of coverage. Are your computers properly covered? Is the limit of insurance adequate? Is a computer virus a covered cause of loss? Does the policy include coverage for laptops and other computer equipment that is away from a bank premises? Is there coverage for PDAs and hand-held computers?

Builder's Risk Insurance

The construction of a new building usually requires specific insurance to address the hazards encountered in construction. Talk with your insurance advisor and contractor about your need for builder's risk insurance.

See chapter three for details on builder's risk insurance.

Property Insurance Exclusions

Most bank property insurance is written on a "special perils" basis. In short, the policy says that every cause of loss is covered except for what is excluded. If the cause of your loss is not excluded, the insurance policy pays.

Here's the normal list of excluded perils:

- ordinance or law
- earth movement
- governmental action
- nuclear hazards
- utility service
- war and military action
- water
- artificially generated electrical currents
- delay, loss of use, and loss of market
- wear and tear, or mechanical breakdown
- changes in temperature or humidity
- explosion of steam boiler or pressure vessel
- continuous or repeated leakage of water
- loss by freezing (unless you take precautions)
- dishonest or criminal acts by you or employees (except for acts of destruction)
- voluntary parting
- rain, snow, ice, or sleet to personal property in the open
- pollution

- acts or decisions
- faulty, inadequate, or defective planning, design, repair, materials, or maintenance

The policy also describes property that is not covered. The excluded items relevant to banks are:

- accounts, bills, currency, money, and notes
- cost of excavations
- foundations, land, and retaining walls
- property covered by another policy
- underground pipes
- fences, radio antennas, and satellite dishes

Vacant Property Issues

A vacant building has coverage restrictions. Most policies say that after a building has been vacant for sixty consecutive days, coverage for the following perils is excluded:

vandalism
sprinkler leakage/water damage
glass breakage
theft or attempted theft

Perhaps the Most Common Bank Property Loss?

Banks don't have a great many property losses. In my career, though, I have seen four banks encounter the same kind of incident. It's a silly event, and the cause of much embarrassment for all concerned: a truck getting stuck in the drive-through teller roof overhang.

Loss prevention is simple for this type of accident. Put up a sign or a hanging tube for the unwary to hit before they hit your building.

Valuable Papers Insurance

Valuable papers insurance pays for the cost of recreating documents destroyed by an insured peril. It pays for the cost of researching and copying the documents you need to run your business after a fire or other insured cause of loss.

Example: A fire destroys part of your office space that contains important loan records. The information is vital both to your operation and to your regulators. The data must be recreated. Valuable papers insurance will pay the restoration costs.

Sidenote: Buying valuable papers insurance alone is a lousy way to protect your bank's records. Physically protect documents or records that are important to your operation. Put your vital documents in fireproof filing cabinets or a vault. Better yet, scan paper records and store them digitally—with proper backup, of course!

Debris Removal

After a fire or other insured damage to your building, there will likely be debris that need to be removed. Coverage is usually limited to 25 percent of the loss. The amounts paid for debris removal do not increase the total limit of coverage for the whole claim. It is, therefore, possible that you can run out of coverage.

To help, insurers provide an additional amount of coverage (usually $10K) to pay for the cleanup. Some insurance companies increase the additional amount to $25K or $50K.

Review your buildings. Will special disposal of rubble and debris increase the cost of reconstruction? Asbestos or other hazardous substances (found in older buildings) may point to the need for additional insurance.

★ Ordinance or Law

After a loss to your building, you may find that local laws and building ordinances increase the cost of reconstruction. Perhaps you will have to add a sprinkler system or handicap access. Recall from our discussion of perils that actions of a government are excluded.

Ordinance or law coverage provides additional insurance to pay for the higher cost of reconstruction due to building codes, laws, or regulations.

The coverage actually has three parts:

Coverage A – Loss to the Undamaged Portion of the Building: Coverage is provided for the value of the part of the building that is undamaged but that must be demolished by order of a governmental authority due to a building code.

Coverage B – Demolition Cost to the Undamaged Portion of the Building: Pays the cost of demolishing and removing the undamaged portion of the building.

Coverage C – Increased Cost of Construction: Pays the increased cost of construction due to law or building codes.

Fine Arts

If your bank owns artwork, antiques, or other items of unusual value, consider having the items appraised and insured under a fine arts policy.

Fine arts insurance provides additional perils (breakage, for example) and alternative valuation methods (cost of restoration) to what is offered by standard insurance policies.

Highly valued windows, murals, and other ornamentation can be specifically insured as well.

Don't forget to insure artwork loaned to museums and galleries. Check the loan agreement; you may find that the receiving institution is responsible for coverage.

Signs

Signs attached to your buildings are covered by most standard building insurance. Freestanding signs need to be insured specifically or with a special policy endorsement.

Mail Insurance

Mail insurance protects property in the custody of a government postal service. Review the policy for specific descriptions of property covered and parties responsible for transporting the property. Some policies will extend coverage to include organizations like FedEx and UPS.

Chapter Three: Builders' Risk Insurance

The builders' risk insurance policy covers buildings during construction, renovation, or repair. Insurance is provided on the structure and materials used in construction. In most cases, materials are covered while in transit, at temporary storage locations, and while stored at the job site.

The following are some of the issues to consider.

Who Is Buying the Coverage?

In many instances, your contractor will obtain the builders' risk coverage for you. Make sure your bank (or the entity that will own the building) is listed as an insured on the policy and that the coverage is broad enough to cover your exposures—specifically soft costs and loss of business income.

You May Already Have Coverage

Your property insurance policy may include coverage for newly acquired and newly constructed buildings. The amount of insurance may be relatively small. However, it may be broad enough to eliminate the need for an additional insurance policy. Talk with your insurance agent and review your policy for the perils included in the coverage.

Amount of Coverage

Most policies require that you use 100 percent of the expected construction cost as the amount of insurance. Coinsurance penalties may apply if you fail to meet this requirement. Work with your insurance advisor to determine what costs to include in selecting the amount of builder's risk coverage. Try to eliminate any coinsurance clause.

Deductibles

Higher deductibles can reduce your insurance costs. Consider $5K, $10K, or more.

Perils Covered

What causes of loss are included in the policy? Special perils insurance forms include damage by any cause except for what's excluded—such as earthquake, flood, intentional damage by you, mold, terrorism, or damage by insects or vermin. Named peril policies list the events that are covered—such as fire, lightning, wind, and explosion. Special perils is preferable because you receive better coverage.

Consider Flood and Earthquake Coverage

Damage caused by flood and earthquake is usually excluded from basic builders' risk policies. Get quotes and consider the additional perils.

Exclusions

In addition to the flood and earthquake exclusions mentioned, most policies will not cover damage caused by defect in construction, defect in design, mold, pollution, settling, cracking, shrinking, bulging, or expansion.

Theft of Building Materials

Some builders' risk insurance policies exclude theft of building materials stored on site. Some require gated storage areas. Read your policy.

Subcontractors' Work

Is the work of subcontractors (while in process) included in the coverage?

Collapse During Construction

Some policies exclude damage caused by the collapse of the building. Review your insurance policy.

Business Income

Coverage can be included for loss of income in the event that a fire or other insured event prevents you from doing business. Imagine a new hotel under construction that is destroyed two months before completion. The losses in revenue while the building is rebuilt could be substantial. Work with your insurance advisor on the correct amount of loss of business income coverage for your bank.

Liability Insurance

Builders' risk insurance does not include coverage for bodily injury or damage to the property of others. Look to your general liability insurance for protection.

Get Quotes

Your insurance agent or broker can get you quotes. For new construction, your agent should get proposals from several insurers. Specialty programs for builders' risk insurance may offer a better price and coverage.

Work with your contractor and architect to determine who should purchase the builders' risk coverage.

Occupancy

Most builders' risk insurance coverage terminates at occupancy. Coverage ends automatically. Be sure to let your agent know ahead of time that you are moving in. Coverage may also terminate if the building is ready for occupancy. Talk with your advisor.

Soft Costs

After a building under construction is destroyed, there may be architects' fees, attorneys' bills, planning board reviews, and the like before reconstruction can begin. Many policies require soft costs to be a separate limit of coverage.

Chapter Four: General Liability Insurance

The purpose of general liability insurance is to provide protection for bodily injury and property damage that comes out of the operation of your bank. The policy will provide coverage for slip and fall claims and other accidents. Most policies also include coverage for personal injury—libel, slander, defamation, and wrongful arrest. Some examples:

A customer falls on your walkway or parking lot.
An employee accidentally injures a customer.
A piece of candy you give away makes a customer sick.
An employee wrongfully accuses a customer of theft.

Occurrence Limit
The general liability insurance policy responds to events that occur during the policy period. The occurrence limit is the coverage amount that is available for each occurrence or accident. One million dollars is the usual minimum limit. Think of this as your limit of coverage for each event.

General Aggregate Limit

The general aggregate limit is the total coverage available for the combination of all occurrences in a policy period. At a minimum, you will want two times your occurrence limit here. Three times is better.

As claims are paid, you use up your aggregate limit. Once the aggregate amount is spent, the policy will no longer pay claims. You will be "out" of insurance.

Products Aggregate Limit

Products liability insurance pays for the bodily injury and property damage that comes from products you sell. The aggregate limit is the most the policy will pay for the combination of all product liability occurrences in a policy period. Buy two or three times the occurrence limit.

★ Personal and Advertising Injury Liability

I usually describe personal injury coverage as protection against lawsuits for hurt feelings. Most policies include coverage in this section for libel, slander, defamation, wrongful eviction, and false arrest.

Advertising injury is coverage for events similar to personal injury items, but occurring specifically in the field of advertising. Coverage is included for infringement of copyright in an advertisement.

The coverage amount is usually the same as the occurrence limit.

★ Damage to Premises Rented to You

This section provides coverage for damage to a building you occupy or rent from others—also called fire legal liability or fire damage liability. The general liability policy excludes damage to property in your care, custody, or control. This section of coverage brings back protection for damage to property you occupy but don't own.

If you rent an office that represents 40 percent of a building, that part of the building is under your control. If your coffee pot causes a fire that destroys the building, your landlord's insurer may (depending on your lease) expect that you will reimburse them for the loss. Your general liability insurance has no trouble paying for the 60 percent you do not control. It's your part of the building that is the problem. Hence the reason for this coverage section.

Most policies provide $100K, but you may need more.

★ Medical Payments

I often call this section of the general liability policy "goodwill insurance." The section provides coverage for medical bills incurred because of an accident at your premises. It pays regardless of fault or liability. The idea is to take care of an injured person's doctor bills quickly, without fuss. Theoretically, fast action should reduce the chances of a lawsuit.

The most common coverage limit is $5K, although more is available.

While this seems like a small amount of coverage, recall that if your negligence caused the accident, you turn to the coverage per occurrence, where the limit is most often $1 million.

"Med pay" is most often used for slip-and-fall accidents.

Exclusions

Here are the common issues not covered by general liability insurance:

pollution (for coverage, buy pollution insurance)
employment practices (discrimination, wrongful discharge)
asbestos, mold, or fungi
contractual liability
employee benefit plan errors (buy fiduciary responsibilities liability insurance)
professional liability (buy professional liability insurance)
injuries to employees (covered by workers' compensation)
automobiles (covered by auto insurance)
aircraft—both owned and non-owned

owned watercraft and non-owned watercraft over twenty-six feet
liquor liability for those in the business of making, selling, or serving alcohol

★ Named Insureds

Review the entities named on your policy to be sure protection is extended to holding companies, subsidiaries, and any charitable foundations managed by your bank.

The best rule of thumb is that if they are not listed on the general liability policy, they are not covered.

★ Employees as Insureds

Most general liability policies include employees, officers, and directors as insureds. Look for the section of your policy that is titled, "Who is an insured."

★ Joint Ventures

Joint ventures with other businesses should have their own insurance program. Most general liability policies exclude outside entities and partnerships. Speak with your insurance advisor.

★ Contractors and Subcontractors

Contractors working for the bank should provide certificates of liability, workers' compensation, and auto liability insurance. This includes plumbers, snowplow operators, electricians, carpenters, landscapers, and HCAC contractors.

Data processing operations and contractors working on your computer systems should provide evidence of professional liability insurance so that you are assured there is coverage for their mistakes that can damage you.

Here is a sample form you can use to enforce certificate requirements:

Contractor Management Process – Certificates Of Insurance – Sample Letter

<<YOUR NAME>>
Insurance Requirements for Outside Contractors and Vendors

_____ (hereinafter "Contractor"), as a condition of our contract of work, agrees to indemnify and hold harmless <<YOUR NAME>> for all claims for property damage and/or damage for personal or bodily injury, including death, which may arise from acts by Contractor, its agents or associates, and its subcontractors and their agents and associates. Contractor agrees to maintain adequate insurance, in form and with companies acceptable to <<YOUR NAME>>, to insure against the aforesaid, as follows:

Type of Insurance	Minimum Limits of Liability
Workers' Compensation	Statutory Limits
General Liability (including contractual liability, completed operations, and contingent liability for acts of subcontractors)	$1 million each occurrence, $2 million aggregate $2 million products/completed operations aggregate
Automobile Liability	$1 million combined single limit
Umbrella Liability Coverage	$3 million

If excavation work is to be completed, no policy may exclude excavation, collapse, or explosion.

Insurance companies must hold a "Best Rating" of an A- or better.

The insurance coverage provided hereunder shall be primary to and non-contributory with any other available insurance of <<YOUR NAME>>. Contractor's general liability and automobile liability insurance policies shall name <<YOUR NAME>> as additional insureds and shall provide <<YOUR NAME>> with a thirty-day notice of cancellation. Certificates of insurance evidencing the above shall be forwarded in advance of any work to:

<<YOUR NAME>>
<<YOUR ADDRESS>>
<<YOUR PHONE NUMBER>>
<<YOUR FAX NUMBER>>
<<YOUR EMAIL ADDRESS>>

Contractor Signature: _____ Date: _____

Name: _____ Title: _____

Contractor Firm Name _____

★ Boats and Planes

Review your bank's use of watercraft and aircraft.

The general liability policy excludes coverage for owned watercraft and non-owed boats over twenty-six feet. Aircraft of any type are excluded (except where you are a fare-paying passenger).

It is not uncommon for banks to host chamber of commerce functions or customer/employee events on large party boats. You may also have loan officers or executives with large boats. Entertaining bank customers or employees may be a normal part of business. If the boat is over twenty-six feet, the bank may be exposed to a lawsuit if an accident occurs.

I have several bank clients who own planes. Using an executive's Cessna to go to a bank association event might put the bank in a situation where there is no liability insurance in case of a crash. Again, talk with your insurance advisor.

★ Pollution Exclusions

Most general liability policies exclude coverage for any form of pollution liability.

The bank's heating oil tank leaks into the neighbor's basement—no coverage.

A gas station the bank owns through a foreclosure has a leaky storage tank—no coverage.

A vacant lot taken in foreclosure is found to be contaminated by industrial waste—no coverage.

Special pollution liability policies are available. Few banks purchase such coverage. Look at your own situation. Identify possible sources of pollution and take action to prevent incidents (regular fuel tank inspections). Review the hazards that exist on properties before you foreclose.

Some attorneys are starting to recommend that banks put REO property into separate entities to protect the bank's assets. That entity (most often a limited liability company) should have its own insurance program—property, general liability. Only your attorney can tell you if this is a valid strategy. It does not solve the insurance problem, but could segregate assets to limit what a claimant can get access to.

★ Construction Defect Exclusions

I've been talking about this issue for a few years now: construction defect.

Here is the scenario. Your bank loans money to a developer for an apartment complex. Prior to completing the project, the developer goes under. You foreclose and sell the project to developer number two, who finishes the buildings and sells them. Two years later, it's found that the windows are improperly installed and that there is $1 million of mold damage that needs to be repaired. As the bank was, during the REO stage, an owner of the property, you get sucked into the suit.

Your general liability policy has no coverage for this exposure. Neither does your lender liability or executive liability.

As with the pollution issue mentioned above, some attorneys are starting to recommend that banks put REO property into separate entities to protect the bank's assets. Again, It does not solve the insurance problem, but could segregate bank assets to limit what a claimant can get access to.

Liability Coverage for Special Events

The general liability insurance policy provides broad protection for bodily injury and damage to the property of others that arise out of your bank's normal operation. Coverage includes both your day-to-day activities and special events such as customer appreciation events, anniversary celebrations, and community event sponsorships. There is generally no need to buy special coverage to protect the bank for these types of parties, assuming that you have adequate limits of insurance.

★ Invasion of Privacy

Violations of privacy become a greater issue almost every day. Look to your general liability insurance for coverage under the personal and advertising injury section for liability that comes from "publication" of private data.

This is no coverage for a data breach.

Most policies will specifically include coverage for "oral or written publication, in any manner, of material that violates a person's right of privacy." There is a standard exclusion for "personal and advertising injury caused by or at the direction of the insured with the knowledge that the act would violate the rights of another and would inflict personal and advertising injury."

Some insurers are adding exclusions to bank insurance for damages caused by an invasion of privacy. Most insurers now offer data breach and privacy liability protection in the directors' and officers' insurance as well as in e-banking liability coverage.

Talk with your insurance advisor.

Chapter Five: Automobile Insurance

The business auto policy covers the bank's exposure to losses from automobiles owned or leased by the bank. It should also cover the bank's liability for damages caused by employees who drive personal vehicles on bank business. Repossessed vehicles and customer-leased and rented vehicles can also be a part of the coverage.

★ Coverage Symbols

Commercial automobile insurance policies specify the extent of coverage provided by using symbols to indicate the breadth of the protection. The declarations page of your auto policy outlines coverage areas (liability, uninsured motorist, medical payments, etc.) with coverage symbols that apply to the type of insurance.

The applicable symbols are numbers 1 through 9. Symbol 1 is the broadest—"any auto." Symbol 9 provides coverage for non-owned vehicles only. Using symbol 7 reduces the coverage to claims from vehicles listed on the policy only. Insurers sometimes use a combination of symbols, 8 and 9 for example, to provide coverage for hired and non-owned autos. Symbol 1 in the liability section would provide coverage for any auto liability claim brought against an insured. Symbol 7 in the liability section would limit liability coverage to claims that come from a vehicle listed on the policy—significantly restricting the coverage.

Commercial Auto Policy Coverage Symbols

The following definitions of the commercial auto symbols are from the ISO commercial auto policy:

1 – Any "Auto."

2 – Owned Autos Only: Only those autos you own (and for liability coverage, any "trailers" you don't own while attached to power units you do own). This includes those autos you acquire ownership of after the policy begins.

3 – Owned Private Passenger Autos Only: Only the private passenger autos you own. This includes those private passenger autos you acquire ownership of after the policy begins.

4 – Owned Autos Other Than Private Passenger Autos Only: Only those autos you own that are not of the private passenger type (and for liability coverage, any trailers you don't own while attached to power units that you do own). This includes those autos not of the private passenger type that you acquire ownership of after the policy begins.

5 – Owned Autos Subject to No-Fault: Only those autos you own that are required to have no-fault benefits in the state where they are licensed or principally garaged. This includes those autos you acquire ownership of after the policy begins, provided that they are required to have no-fault benefits in the state where they are licensed or principally garaged.

6 – Owned Autos Subject to a Compulsory Uninsured Motorists Law: Only those autos you own that, because of the law in the state where they are licensed or principally garaged, are required to have and cannot reject uninsured motorists coverage. This includes those autos you acquire ownership of after the policy begins, provided they are subject to the same state uninsured motorists requirement.

7 – Specifically Described Autos: Only those autos described in item three of the declarations for which a premium charge is shown (and for liability coverage, any trailers you don't own while attached to any power unit described in item three).

8 – Hired Autos Only: Only those autos you lease, hire, rent, or borrow. This does not include any auto you lease, hire, rent, or borrow from any of your employees, partners (if you are a partnership), members (if you are a limited liability company), or members of their households.

9 – Non-owned Autos Only: Only those autos you do not own, lease, hire, rent, or borrow that are used in connection with your business. This includes autos owned by your employees, partners (if you are a partnership), members (if you are a limited liability company), or members of their households, but only while used in your business or personal affairs.

From ISO form BA0001 10 01 – Copyright ISO Properties, Inc. 2000

Automobile Liability

This part of your auto insurance provides protection for the injuries you cause (bodily injury) and the damage you do to other people's property (property damage) in the use or ownership of motor vehicles. The most common limit of coverage is $1 million.

The preferred coverage symbol is 1, "any auto." Some insurers insist on using symbol 7 (Specifically Described Autos), symbol 8 (Hired Autos Only), and symbol 9 (Non-owned Autos Only). The coverage is, in substance, the same.

Uninsured Motorists/Underinsured Motorists

Uninsured/underinsured motorists insurance pays for the injuries to you and others in your car caused by a driver who either has no insurance or too little insurance. Your insurer pays you then "goes after" the other person.

Coverage availability varies by state. In most cases, it is best to have the limit of uninsured motorist coverage the same as your liability coverage. Recall that injured employees (while working) are most often covered by workers' compensation insurance.

★ Personal Injury Protection

Personal injury protection is also known as "no-fault" or PIP insurance. Puerto Rico and twelve states operate under a no-fault system where those injured in an auto accident are limited in monetary damages they can recover from a driver who causes an accident. In such states, PIP pays for your medical bills caused by an auto accident. Under no-fault, you don't need to sue the other party.

Medical Payments

Medical payments coverage pays the medical bills for people in your vehicle when there are injuries in an accident. In most states, this coverage is limited to some relatively small amount—$1K or $5K. It can be used to pay the deductibles and co-payments of your health insurance.

Comprehensive

Comprehensive coverage is also called "other than collision." This part of your auto insurance pays for the damage to your car caused by something other than an accident—fire, hail, windstorm, theft, or vandalism, for example. The coverage section also pays for the damage to your car caused by hitting an animal, as such is not considered an accident but an "act of God."

There is usually a deductible stated—the amount you pay in the event of an accident.

Use a large deductible to control premiums. Consider removing comprehensive coverage if your vehicle is more than five model years old.

Collision

Collision insurance pays for the damage to your car or truck that has been in an accident—collision with other vehicles, objects, people, even the surface of the road. Some policies call the coverage "collision and upset" to reinforce the broad range of accidents included. The accident could be your fault or that of another driver. Your vehicle could be unattended and roll down a hill.

A deductible reduces the amount of the payment made by your insurance company. Increase your deductible and you reduce your premium.

Consider removing collision coverage if your vehicle is more than five model years old.

Towing & Labor Insurance

Pays for the cost of towing and labor expenses when your vehicle is disabled. Usually limited to some small amount—$35, for example. This is usually not worth the premium. Don't turn in small property claims!

Rental Vehicle Coverage

Pays for the rental of a car after an accident. Coverage is usually limited to some amount per day with a total coverage maximum.

This is another area of low severity. It may be a part of an extension endorsement provided by your insurer.

Auto Extension Endorsements

Many insurers have a policy endorsement that extends protection to many different areas. Coverage can include life insurance, additional medical payments, payments for remaining lease installments, and extensions of the coverage for a car you rent. Talk with your agent about your particular policy.

★ Non-Owned Auto Coverage/Liability From Employees Driving

It isn't just the cars you own that expose your bank to liability. Every time an employee goes to a meeting or visits with a customer, the bank is exposed. If a loan officer causes an accident while driving his own vehicle on bank business, the bank could be sued.

Employees driving on bank business are the largest risk for catastrophic loss most banks face. In the blink of an eye, a VP or teller could cause an accident involving a school bus or multiple vehicles. No other area of liability puts your bank at such high risk.

Check with your agent to be sure you have non-owned auto coverage.

★ Drive Other Car Coverage

There is a significant gap in the coverage provided by the commercial auto policy. Employees who buy personal auto insurance do not have to worry about this gap.

The problem arises when an employee (or spouse) is provided with a bank vehicle as their only vehicle.

Personal insurance extends coverage for the insured driving a vehicle owned by a third party (a neighbor, for example). The commercial auto policy does not provide such an expansion of coverage.

Drive other car coverage, added to the commercial auto policy, protects employees who are provided company cars and don't have their own personal auto policy. Coverage is broadened to include the employee while he is driving another vehicle.

If your bank provides employees with vehicles for personal use, discuss this exposure with your insurance advisor.

★ When Your Employees Rent Cars

When renting cars (short-term rentals from the well-known rental car companies located at every airport), either buy the coverage offered by the rental car company or use a credit card that provides the same insurance. Call your credit card customer service department for the details of your credit card company's service.

The issue is not that your business auto policy is inadequate. The problem is the requirements and hassles that the credit card company will put you through. It is simply not worth the $15 or $20 a day rental car companies will charge you for the insurance. Frankly, it's almost extortion. Here is my take on what the rental car companies say in their rental agreements:

Dear Rental Car Customer,

You are free to buy our collision damage waiver coverage. If you buy it, you can drop the keys on our counter and walk away from any responsibility to us for accidental damage.

Should you decide not to buy our coverage, here is what we are going to do:

1. We will tag your credit card for our estimate of the damages to our car. You will have no appeal or say in how much we charge you. Even the most minor damage will be at least $5K. Because we can.

2. Our fee for the damage to our car will be based on the replacement cost of the vehicle. No, not the cost to repair the damage, the cost to replace the car. We know that your insurance pays only for the cost of repair. We do not care.

3. We will charge you our highest rental fee for every day our car is not available to rent. We are the judge of the time our car is out of commission. You pay our rate even if we take our sweet time fixing our car.

4. If your credit card does not have enough limit to pay these expenses, we will call the law on you. You may have heard that we have actually had the local sheriff pull people off of planes when we could not verify adequate credit card limits. We will neither confirm nor deny that story.

5. We do not care what kind of insurance you have. The above rules apply. We leave it to you to collect what you can from your insurer, when you can collect it. (We also wish you good luck in doing so.)

Sincerely,
Almost Every Rental Car Company

★ Employees as Insureds

The basic commercial auto policy provides coverage only for the named insured. In other words, the bank is protected. No insurance is provided to the employee driving the vehicle. Employees as insureds is an endorsement that extends coverage specifically to employees.

★ Damage to Employee Vehicles

What are the employees' expectations for damage caused in accidents while driving their personal vehicles? Will you pay for damage to their vehicle, or should the employee rely upon his own insurance? Will you pay his deductible?

Make your plan clear in your employee handbook to avoid misunderstandings. Send an annual reminder to all employees stating your bank's policy on employee vehicle usage.

Here's a sample letter you can use:

Dear Employee,

From time to time, it may be necessary for you to drive your personal vehicle on bank business. The purpose of this letter is to remind/advise you of our policy regarding such.

All employees using their personal vehicles for approved business travel will be reimbursed for such use at a rate of <$.xx> per mile. This fee is intended to repay you for your expenses in operating the vehicle, including the cost of gas, oil, tires, maintenance, and the cost of insurance.

We require that all employees who drive personal vehicles on bank business carry at least <$x00,000> of liability protection and uninsured motorist coverage. The purchase of "comprehensive" and collision insurance is at your discretion.

In the event of an accident while you are driving on bank business, you should look to your own insurance to protect you and your vehicle.

Remember, the auto insurance you buy is what will protect you on or off company time. Our bank automobile insurance policy provides no coverage for your vehicle.

Should you have any questions regarding this memo, please see your supervisor.

Use the Same Insurer for Auto and General Liability

Consider having the same insurer for auto and general liability to eliminate any coverage gaps or overlaps. There are times when an event falls in a gray area between auto liability and general liability insurance. It is good practice to have one insurer who provides you with both areas of coverage.

Repossessed Vehicles

How are repossessed cars covered by your auto insurance policy? "Any auto" liability coverage will protect the bank (see prior discussion on auto policy symbols).

How about damage to the repossessed vehicles—comprehensive and collision insurance? A repossessed vehicle is considered an owned vehicle by most insurers. You may be able to add coverage to your bank's auto policy.

You may have coverage on your lenders' single interest insurance policy (see chapter fourteen). Talk with your agent.

Parking Garages

Is the exposure for your parking garage or parking lot covered? Providing parking may expose the bank to claims for damage that occurs to customers' cars. This is certainly true if you charge a fee for parking.

What are the employees' expectations of payment for damage to their vehicles while parked in the bank's parking lot? Talk with your agent about your need for special coverage, known as garagekeeper's insurance.

Chapter Six: Workers' Compensation

Workers' compensation insurance is required by most states. Protection is provided for employees injured in the conduct of their work. Workers are covered at the bank, during customer meetings, while driving to business appointments, and at conventions and conferences. Employees are eligible for work comp benefits regardless of who caused the injury and regardless of the stupidity of the action that caused the injury.

Your bank pays a premium based on your payroll and past loss experience. The insurance company handles any claims that occur. The detail of the premium calculation is where there are opportunities for mistakes and savings.

★ Importance of Correct Classification

Review your policy classifications for accuracy. Work with your agent to be sure that the classes and rates you have are correct for your operation. Ask your agent for a copy of the Scopes® description of your classifications. Most bank employees will be classified as "clerical." Maintenance and courier drivers will be separately rated. There also may be a separate sales code for commercial lenders and other marketing people who are on the road.

Common Workers' Compensation Employment Classifications for Banks

Clerical: tellers, receptionists, secretaries, loan processors, and office workers

Sales: commercial lenders who regularly visit customers

Drivers: couriers and drivers

Building Operations By Owner or Real Estate Company: Professional employees

Building Operations By Owner or Real Estate Company: Other employees, such as janitors

Understand the Definition of Payroll

Make sure your insurer isn't charging you for payroll that should not be included. For example, the extra wages you pay for overtime work should be removed. Your executive officers' payrolls may be eligible for capping at a maximum wage. Talk with your insurance advisor.

Get Copies of Your Audit Worksheets

Ask your insurer to provide you with a copy of the audit worksheet prepared for your most recently expired policy. This document provides the details of how the insurance company determined your final premium. It lists employees, classifications, and payrolls. Look for errors such as the inclusion of overtime and incorrect classification of employees.

Consider Deductibles

Consider using a substantial deductible to control your premiums. Work with your agent to determine the effect that deductibles will have on your costs and your future experience modification.

Experience Modification

Most banks have, as part of the premium calculation, a factor that is a ratio of expected losses to actual losses. This factor is known as an experience modification. Ask your agent to work with you to review your experience modification worksheet for accuracy. Check the payrolls and losses that are a part of the calculation.

A modification of 1.0 indicates that your losses are average. An experience modification of 1.2 means that your losses are higher than average. A modification of .89 is reflective of loss experience better than average. Your experience modification factor is multiplied by your gross premium, so a 1.2 mod increases your costs by 20 percent.

Many banks seem to be satisfied with an experience modification that hovers around 1.0. Some commentators have said that a mod at this level is the equivalent of a school grade of C. Most would agree that this is nothing to write home about.

To objectively judge your modification, determine your "perfect" mod—the mod you would carry if you experienced no losses. (Your agent should be able to provide you with info on your perfect mod. If not, call me and let's find you a new insurance agent.) The difference between your experience modification and your perfect modification indicates the part of the modification to control.

For example, if your mod is .98 and you determine that your perfect mod is .74, you then know that .24 of your experience mod is your fault. No losses would mean a reduction in your mod of the .24. You can also use this information to determine what your losses cost you in additional premiums.

Controlling your experience modification is a function of your efforts to control your loss frequency and the severity of losses you have. It also is a function of claims management. (See chapter twenty-nine.)

Your Perfect Mod

Your workers' compensation experience modification is the ratio of your expected losses to your actual losses. Your perfect mod is the experience modification you would have if there were no losses on your record.

Figuring out the difference between your current experience mod and the perfect mod tells you the impact *your* claims have on *your* premium. Contact me for a report showing your mod, your perfect mod, and the impact that loss severity and frequency has on your claims: Scott@ ScottSimmonds.com.

Employers' Liability

This is the second (often ignored) part of the workers' compensation insurance policy. It covers the employer from bodily injury liability arising out of the employment relationship—but not injuries to employees.

In my career, I have seen two claims in employers' liability. Neither was from banking exposures, but they serve to illustrate the coverage.

The first was a construction risk where a wife brought lunch to her husband at a job site. On arrival at the site, she witnessed her husband falling to his death. She claimed emotional distress at seeing the accident.

The second claim was in a boat-building operation where a father's work clothing was contaminated with fiberglass particles. The clothing was washed in the family laundry, where the children picked up the fibers and got sick.

In the banking world, claims could come from a spouse's claim of loss of companionship or services after an employee's injury.

Limits of Coverage for Employers' Liability

Typical limits of coverage:

Each accident: $100K
Disease: policy limit $500K
Disease: each employee $100K

Some umbrella insurers require higher limits of coverage:

Each accident: $500K
Disease: policy limit $500K
Disease: each employee $500K

Some specialty programs and self-insured workers' compensation plans will have available limits of $1 million.

Chapter Seven: Umbrella Liability

The commercial umbrella liability policy provides liability coverage in addition to your general liability, auto liability, and employers' liability (part of the workers' comp policy).

Umbrella Coverage Example

If you have a $5 million umbrella policy and an auto liability policy with $1 million of coverage, the total amount of protection you have for an auto accident is $6 million.

Underlying Coverage

Do the limits of coverage for your underlying policies meet the umbrella requirements? Each umbrella policy will outline the coverage limits for the underlying policies. Failure to meet these limits may mean a gap in coverage between the liability coverage and the umbrella.

Standard Underlying Insurance Requirements for Umbrella Liability

Auto Liability	$1 million
General Liability	$1 million per occurrence
	$3 million aggregate
Employers' Liability	$500K each accident
	$500K disease – policy limit
	$500K disease – each employee

Concurrence of Policy Dates

Are the policy dates of your underlying policies the same as the umbrella policy? Having a single date prevents the problems of missing a renewal date and issues of aggregate limits of coverage.

Mental Anguish

Are mental injury and mental anguish a part of the policy definition of bodily injury in your umbrella policy? Many policies define bodily injury as only when there is a physical injury. Claims of emotional distress are certainly not uncommon.

I often get pushback from insurance agents on this coverage. About half of the insurers seem to offer "mental injury as bodily injury" coverage. They all should. (Email me if your insurer refuses to add mental injury as bodily injury coverage. I can provide copies of endorsements other insurers have used.)

Multiple Liability Policies

If you have more than one general liability policy, be sure your umbrella policy applies as excess coverage over each. (While I can't think of a good reason why a bank would have more than one general liability policy, I quite often see where an insurance agent has purchased separate business owner's insurance policies for leased branch buildings. I can't explain why this is done—I just know I see it fairly often.)

Personal Injury Exclusions

Review the definitions and exclusions relative to personal injury. You may find additional exclusions in your umbrella policy or different definitions from those in the underlying policies. Internet marketing activities may be excluded or limited.

Review your umbrella policy exclusions. The coverage may be more restrictive than your primary policies.

Coverage Limits

The limit of umbrella liability coverage you buy for your bank will depend on the size of your bank, where you're located, and the cost of coverage. I consider $5 million to be the minimum for even the smallest bank. Get quotes at various limits of coverage so you can judge the value of higher limits.

★ Common Exclusions

Your umbrella policy will have exclusions similar to those on your general liability and auto policy. Here are some of the exclusions that will probably be listed on your insurance:

- pollution (for coverage, buy pollution insurance)
- employment practices—such as discrimination or wrongful discharge
- asbestos, mold, or fungi
- contractual liability
- employee benefit plan errors (buy fiduciary responsibilities liability insurance)

- professional liability (buy professional liability insurance)
- injuries to employees (covered by workers' compensation)
- aircraft—both owned and non-owned
- owned watercraft and non-owned watercraft over twenty-six feet
- liquor liability for those in the business of making, selling, or serving alcohol

Chapter Eight: ★ Introduction to Lender Asset Protection Insurance

I use "lender asset protection insurance" to describe those insurance policies that protect a lender's interest in the property that it holds as collateral for loans.

Here are the policies included in lender asset protection insurance:

<u>Mortgage Errors and Omissions Insurance</u> – Protects the bank from errors made in the management of the collateral or government guarantees that support a mortgage.

<u>Forced-Placed/Foreclosed Property Insurance</u> – Property insurance covering either properties the bank owns or properties the bank has a mortgage interest in when the owner has failed to buy insurance.

<u>Forced-Placed/Foreclosed Flood Insurance</u> – Property insurance covering flood either at properties the bank owns or properties the bank has a mortgage interest in when the owner has failed to buy insurance.

<u>Real Estate Owned Liability Insurance</u> – Bodily injury and property damage liability insurance protecting the bank from lawsuit by a third party.

<u>Lenders' Single Interest Insurance</u> – Coverage on the lender's interest in cars, boats, trucks, motorcycles, and other chattel held as security in a loan.

These policies are often provided by specialty lines insurers and insurance agents who specialize in this area of coverage.

Banks often have the loan department manage lender protection insurance policies instead of the chief risk officer or chief financial officer.

I urge you to have a single agent for your bank's entire lender asset protection insurance. The coverages are complex and need to be made to work together. A specialist in these coverages is important to proper functioning. Two agents I have found to be exceptional are The Miniter Group (<u>www.Miniter.com</u>) and the firm Lee and Mason (<u>www.LeeAndMason.com</u>).

Chapter Nine: Mortgage Errors and Omissions Insurance

Mortgage errors and omissions insurance protects the bank from errors made in the management of the collateral or government guarantees that support a mortgage.

There are several different versions of the policy. Some are stand-alone., as in a separate policy Some are included in the bank's insurance package policy (along with the bank's building insurance and general liability insurance).

Mortgage Impairment

This section protects your interest in a mortgage from a physical damage loss (e.g., fire, lightning, wind, etc.) as a result of "required" perils when your customer has not kept insurance in force or has not properly insured the property.

Mortgage Impairment Example

A mortgage customer allows his or her homeowner's insurance to lapse. Your loan department is not aware of the cancellation. The home is in a fire, leveling the structure. The loan goes into default. Mortgage impairment insurance protects the bank against loss of the outstanding loan amount.

Most policies respond to the perils (causes of loss) required in the mortgage agreement. If the loan requires "fire, extended coverage, and vandalism," then the mortgage impairment policy responds only to those perils. The insurance responds to the coverage required by your mortgage.

Some mortgage impairment policies require that the bank tracks and checks customer insurance policies. Some require regular notice to customers of the mortgage requirement to purchase insurance. Some don't require any form of tracking customer insurance policies, saving the bank a great deal of effort and administrative expense.

Most policies limit coverage for a set time from the date you are aware of a lapse in the insurance—usually ninety days. This allows you time to place coverage in your "forced-placed" property insurance program. (See See chapters ten and eleven for forced-placed coverage.)

Non-Required Perils or Balance of Perils

This additional coverage supplements the perils covered by the first part of the mortgage impairment policy. Don't overlook the importance of this section. Your mortgage's required perils may not include damage by weight of ice and snow, vandalism, frozen pipes, water damage, or building collapse. Coverage can also be included here for flood and earthquake.

Mortgagee's Errors and Omissions

Coverage for errors in the administration of escrowed insurance premiums or in the various government guarantee programs—VHA, GNMA, SBA, etc.

The policy may include mistakes in determining the flood map location of the property. Failure to administer property tax payments properly for the customer is also a part of many policies.

General Comments

There is no universal mortgage errors and omissions policy language. Each insurer's policy is unique, with distinctive terms and conditions. You need to read and understand your policy.

Be sure the perils included in your coverage are broad in nature. Consider adding flood and earthquake to the policy.

Some insurers exclude mobile homes from coverage on the basic policy. You can purchase the coverage for an additional premium.

Most mortgage errors and omissions policies require that you obtain proof that insurance is in place at the time the mortgage is closed. You can do nothing that would lead a mortgage customer to believe he or she doesn't need to buy insurance.

Some mortgage impairment policies require that you annually provide a written notice to customers that insurance is required as a condition of the mortgage.

Review your policy to see if you are required to maintain proof of insurance coverage. Most policies now only require action at the time you are notified that coverage has been cancelled. So-called "non-checking" policies allow your loan department to ignore renewal notices and precancellation notices. You can even ignore the cancellation notices for several weeks, enough time for late-paying customers to have their policies reinstated.

Non-checking policies allow your loan department to hold off on any action for as long as ninety days from the date you know that a policy has been cancelled. Many banks use a sixty-day schedule; they follow up on policies that have not been reinstated sixty days from cancellation. That gives them plenty of time to put coverage into place on the "forced-placed" insurance program if need be.

Mortgage-Impairment vs. Mortgage-Hazard Insurance

There is a fair amount of confusion by bankers over the two types of insurance coverage that protect the bank against customers who fail to buy insurance on their mortgaged properties—mortgage-impairment insurance and mortgage-hazard insurance.

The coverage is different. The triggers of payment under the policies are different. The premiums are different.

Mortgage-impairment covers the mortgage.

Mortgage-hazard covers the mortgaged property.

Note the difference.

Mortgage-impairment covers the mortgage to the extent that the mortgage becomes "impaired" due to direct physical loss or another covered incident. Said another way, the loss is a default of the mortgage due to a covered incident that damages the mortgaged property.

Mortgage-hazard is direct property insurance coverage for a building; the insurance loss is triggered by damage the building. The policy does not care if there is a mortgage default. A loss to the building prompts a payment following the terms of the insurance policy.

Mortgage-hazard is broader coverage and provides more flexibility to the bank. It is better than mortgage-impairment insurance in most cases. It is also more expensive.

Mortgage-Hazard Insurance

Mortgage-hazard insurance responds to a property loss that takes place at the mortgaged property when that loss is not covered by insurance. Unlike mortgage-impairment insurance, foreclosure does not have to take place for the mortgage-hazard insurance to pay.

The bank may pay for the repair of the property and add the repair costs to the current loan. They may foreclose, but they don't have to.

Again, foreclosure is *not* precedent to coverage under the mortgage-hazard policy. The policy responds to an otherwise uninsured physical damage loss (e.g., fire, wind, hail, etc.) to the covered property. It is the bank's option as to when to use this coverage as first-party coverage. Damages or premiums do not have to be billed back to the borrower.

Mortgage-Hazard Example: A customer of the bank fails to renew his or her insurance. A fire damages the property. The customer cannot pay to repair the damage.

The bank submits the claim to the insurer based on the damage done to the property. The bank may have the property repaired and add the damage amount to the current mortgage, allowing the mortgage customer to stay in his or her home. The bank may "forgive" the loss amount, or it may go to foreclosure and take over the property.

The disposition of the mortgage is up to the bank. The bank's loss in value due to the loss to the property is paid by the mortgage-hazard policy. The policy allows for flexibility in action by the bank.

	Mortgage-Impairment	Mortgage-Hazard
Protects the bank's interest in mortgaged property when the mortgage customer fails to buy insurance.	Yes	Yes
Responds to damage to mortgaged property.	After foreclosure precipitated by property damage.	Yes
Requires liquidation.	Yes	No
Requires that the bank track insurance.	At bank's option as declared in policy.	No
Requires that the bank force-place coverage if a property is found to be without insurance.	**Yes**	**No**
Policy responds to perils required by mortgage.	**Yes**	**Yes**

Chapter Ten: Forced-Placed/Foreclosed Property Insurance

Once it has been discovered that a mortgaged property is not insured by the mortgagee, coverage must be "placed" in force by the bank.

Most bank mortgage errors and omissions policies (see the prior section of this book) allow ninety days to place alternate coverage from the time it is discovered that an insurance policy has lapsed. Forced-placed policies are one way to insure a customer's property when the customer fails to obtain insurance. The amount of coverage is usually the amount of the outstanding loan. Banks can (in most states) charge the premium back to the customer's account, though proposed regulation is threatening this practice.

Most forced-placed policies are on a reporting form. The insurance company charges a minimum deposit premium ($500 for a small- to medium-sized bank is not unusual), and reports of the property to be covered are made each month to the insurance company. The deposit is used up as the reports of property covered accumulate. Insurers then bill an additional premium to the bank.

Be aware of the perils that are insured, and the penalties for missed reports. Also, coverage for foreclosed properties can usually be added to most policies at a different (more costly) premium rate.

Some smaller banks are able to place the property insurance through a local agent. This tends to involve more administrative work on the bank's part, as each property will be individually underwritten by an insurer. There also may be restrictions to coverage for loss by vandalism when a property is vacant and covered by a standard policy.

A great number of forced-placed property insurance includes a provision that provides automatic coverage when a customer is found to have no insurance. This can almost act as retroactive insurance—being put in force after a loss has occurred. This coverage feature is usually a part of policies where the agent managing the forced-placed policy has taken over the insurance tracking work for the bank.

Because of the cost of insurance tracking and the administrative issues put on banks by regulation, more banks are considering "blanket mortgage hazard" insurance that eliminates all tracking and forced-placing of insurance. Banks buy a policy that covers the actual loss of a mortgaged property when the borrower's insurance fails to respond. With this policy, nobody tracks insurance or force-places insurance. Obviously, this policy is not inexpensive. Some banks, however, are finding it a valid approach.

Chapter Eleven: ★ Forced-Placed Flood Insurance

This coverage is usually a separate policy to the forced-placed property insurance.

As has been mentioned here before, the peril of flood is not covered by standard property insurance. You need a separate policy. Same with forced-placed.

The basic coverage offered by most insurers who provide forced-placed flood insurance is $250K on residential properties and $500K on commercial buildings. Also, beware that most of these policies do not include coverage on the contents of a building and may have limitations as to coverage on property or damage to basements or other property below ground level.

These policies are usually monthly reporting forms. You tell the insurers what properties you need to cover and pay an adjusted premium each month.

Chapter Twelve: ★ Real Estate Owned Liability Insurance

This policy is general liability coverage for your foreclosed property—serving as protection from bodily injury and property damage lawsuits against the bank. Claims examples include (1) a real estate agent falls through the floor of the house while he or she is showing it, (2) a child is injured playing in the back yard, or (3) a visitor falls in the driveway.

I prefer that the bank's general liability insurance (the same policy that covers bank branches and parking lots) covers foreclosed properties. You get broader coverage and the protection of the umbrella liability policy. Most insurance agents selling REO property insurance almost automatically add liability coverage. Get this exposure covered on your bank's general liability policy and cancel the separate REO liability policy.

Chapter Thirteen: ★ Insurance Tracking Services

The importance of protecting the bank's collateral is indisputable. Tracking insurance is a big part of a lender's administration work. There are renewal notices, cancellation notices, payment notices, and mortgage customers who change insurance companies. Someone has to watch what is going on.

The mortgage errors and omissions policy mentioned chapter nine covers the bank when tracking fails and an insurance falls through the cracks.

More and more banks are considering outsourced tracking services—usually from the organization that provides the forced-placed insurance.

As I write this, there is a great deal of concern over the forced-placed insurance business and changes required by various bank regulators and regulations. Premiums charged by banks when they place insurance coverage for a customer are under scrutiny. Tracking services and the fees charged (or not charged) to banks for services are a part of what regulators are looking at.

Regulators seem to see the premiums charged to mortgage customers who fail to meet their mortgage terms by buying insurance as a profit center for banks. Insurers and agents who provide the forced-placed coverage are seen as gouging insureds. Regulators are looking at all aspects of the transaction to see where and if banks are making profits on these policies or realizing reduced expenses by allowing insurers to track policies.

Chapter Fourteen: ★ Lender's Single Interest Insurance Policies

Lender's single interest insurance protects the bank from loss or damage to personal property that is the collateral for loans—cars, trucks, boats, RVs, snowmobiles, and other personal property. Coverage is provided for the bank's interest and not that of the borrower.

Be careful of the potential coverage overlap of lender's single interest with the mortgage impairment insurance on mobile homes.

Coverage is usually included for repossessed property. Policies can include protection for title errors and omissions as well.

Most lender single interest policies are paid on a monthly reporting basis. The bank reports the value of secured loans, and a premium is charged for the exposure.

Coverage can include repossession expense reimbursement, mechanic's lien reimbursement, gap/deficiency coverage, borrower deductible coverage, and vehicle location/skip reimbursement.

Lender's single interest is usually sold by specialty insurers. Bank trade associations often have access to special programs.

Chapter Fifteen: Unique Issues of Claims-Made Policies

Before we get into the directors' and officers' policy (D&O) or the employment practices liability policy, let's review the components of claims-made insurance.

Most casualty insurance policies (general liability, automobile, workers' compensation) pay for events that occur during the policy period. For example, an auto insurance policy will pay for an accident that occurs while the policy is in force. D&O policies, however, pay for lawsuits filed during the policy period; the wrongful act could have occurred years before. Claims-made policies respond only when a suit is filed or when a strong threat of a suit exists.

Difference between Claims-Made and Occurrence Policies

Claims-made policy: pays based on the date of the lawsuit.

Occurrence policy: pays based on the date of the accident or occurrence.

Retroactive Date

Claims-made policies respond to claims brought during the policy period. Some policies include a requirement that the occurrence (the date of the wrongful act) takes place after the "retroactive date." When changing insurance companies, it is vital to understand if the new policy has a retro date. The use of a "tail" may be necessary if the retro date is not sufficiently in the past.

★ Pending and Prior Litigation Exclusions

Most policies now do not include the above-described retroactive date. Instead, insurers cut off coverage for any claim that was known prior to the inception of the policy. So-called "pending and prior" dates serve to protect the insurer from the insured claiming coverage when that person already knew the "barn was on fire," so to speak. Such pending and prior exclusions allow the insured to have full comfort in coverage for prior acts.

Warning!

The downside of a claims-made policy comes if the policy is cancelled.

Example: A D&O policy is put in force January 1, 2010, and is renewed in 2011 and 2012. In 2013, however, the bank decides to end the coverage, as the premium has increased. Six months later, a letter from an attorney arrives announcing a lawsuit for discrimination in hiring that occurred in 2011. No coverage. Although the policy was in force at the time of the alleged discrimination, the policy was not in force when the suit was filed.

The solution to the above problem is to keep policies in force. Short of that, you will need the extended reporting period found in most policies (see the next paragraph).

Why would any bank cancel its D&O insurance? Mergers and acquisitions are the most common reason. Perhaps claim problems prevent a new insurer from providing coverage for past acts?

Discovery Period/Tail/Reporting Period

Claims-made policies provide protection for lawsuits and actions brought during the policy period. In the event that coverage is replaced or cancelled, protection may be desired for events that took place prior to expiration/ cancellation but for which no claim has yet been filed. This is called a "tail" or "extended reporting period."

Issues to Consider in Your Current Policies:

Can the insured buy the extended reporting period (ERP) at his or her option, or only when the insurance company cancels the policy?

For what time period is the extension of reporting valid? You may want at least three years of coverage.

What is the premium for the ERP?

In what time frame must the insured decide to buy the ERP?

Chapter Sixteen: Executive Risk/Directors' and Officers' Insurance

Some of you will have jumped right to this section. Welcome!

The directors' and officers' insurance policy (D&O) was originally designed to protect the directors and officers from allegations of mismanagement and bad decisions. Over the last twenty years, the policy has evolved to include a wide range of exposures, from fiduciary and entity coverage to employment practices liability insurance. It is really much more accurate to call these policies "executive risk insurance," for they actually protect organizations and executives from a wide range of decision-based exposures.

There are no standard D&O insurance policies. Coverage provided varies widely by insurer. Each policy and proposal of coverage must be reviewed and analyzed carefully to determine the best offering based upon the needs of the financial institution.

Summary of Coverage

Bank directors and officers have a fiduciary responsibility to customers, shareholders, and the general public in all dealings. They must work to the interests of the stakeholders in their dealings. There are also regulatory issues.

A prime purpose of directors' and officers' insurance is to protect the personal assets of the directors, officers, and employees of a financial institution from losses arising from "wrongful acts."

Each insurer's policy has a unique definition of "wrongful act." The term refers to any actual or alleged act, omission, error, misstatement, misleading statement, instance of neglect, or breach of duty by an "insured person" in the discharge of his or her duties with the financial institution.

"Insured persons" are (generally) any past, present, or future director, officer, employee, or honorary director or trustee of the financial institution.

Losses include any amount that the insured persons are legally obligated to pay, including judgments, settlements, defense costs, pre- and post-judgment interest, and punitive damages (where insurable by law). Fines and civil money penalties are almost never covered by insurance—without special endorsements.

Pure D&O policies do not provide protection for the "entity," the bank itself. Many lawsuits name one or more "insured persons" as well as the bank. In such a case, without entity coverage in a D&O policy, judgments, settlements, and costs of defense will be allocated by the insurer between the financial institution and the individual insured persons. If the allocation determines that 60 percent of the action was attributable to an insured person, the D&O policy (without entity coverage) would pay only 60 percent of the judgment. The balance would not be covered.

Today's broad executive risk policies include entity protection, making the D&O policy a broad "errors & omissions" type of contract with coverage for: securities-related suits

- shareholder suits
- lending-related suits brought by borrowers or guarantors
- suits brought by depositors alleging negligence with regard to any kind of forgery, unauthorized withdrawal, or employee dishonesty
- suits related to electronic banking activities
- suits related to IRA or Keogh plan administration

- suits alleging breach of fiduciary duty or employee benefit plan liability
- suits alleging notary errors and omissions
- suits alleging negligence regarding investment advice
- suits related to data processing operations performed by the financial institution

- suits brought by business partners
- suits served against the bank by third parties wronged by business partners or scam artists, alleging that the bank is negligent simply by virtue of being the perpetrator's depository
- nuisance suits initiated by those who go after the "deep pockets" of the financial institution

D&O policies also can include protection for "employment-related practices" such as discrimination, wrongful discharge, sexual harassment, and the like.

Indemnification

The idea that D&O protects directors and officers is actually a bit off. In most claims, D&O reimburses the bank for the bank's indemnification of the officers and directors.

Your bank's bylaws include an indemnification agreement that requires the bank to reimburse directors for expenses incurred in their duties. In reality, it is the assets of your bank that protect your officers and directors. Your D&O insurance reimburses your bank.

No Standard Coverage

As there are no standard D&O policies, each policy and proposal must be evaluated on its own merits. No two policies use the same definitions or exclusions.

Claims-Made Policy

See chapter fifteen on claims-made policy issues.

Policy Limit

What amount of coverage is provided by the insurance policy? What is the total amount of protection offered for the total of all claims during the covered time frame (also known as an aggregate limit)? D&O policies are "claims-made contracts." Coverage applies to any claim brought during the policy period. Multiple claims can, in effect, use up the limit of coverage.

Many factors must be considered when deciding what policy limits your institution should carry: price, terms of the policy, peer data, regulatory requirements, and capital levels. Almost every banker wants to know how much insurance they should buy. It's an unanswerable question. However, I'll try...

Each year I put out an update of my recommended minimum limits of insurance for banks. Go to www.UofBankInsurance.Com for the latest edition.

★ Aggregate Policy Limits, Separate Limits, or Both

Each policy has limits on the dollars that will be paid out. Coverage is changed dramatically by the structure of the limit. Does the policy have an aggregate maximum, a total limit of all claims? Do claims in one section deplete limits of coverage available in other coverage sections?

Examples:

Suppose you have an a policy with an aggregate limit of $3 million, a D&O limit of $3 million, an entity limit of $2 million, and an employment practices limit of $1 million. Here, employment practices claims reduce the coverage available for claims against the directors and officers.

Then consider a policy with no aggregate limit, a D&O limit of $3 million, an entity limit of $2 million, and an employment practices limit of $1 million. In this example, claims in one part of the coverage do not impact the coverage available.

Entity Coverage Included in Policy Limit

While entity coverage is an important protection, improperly designed coverage can dilute the insurance available for true D&O claims. If claims in the entity section of coverage reduce the limits available, the bank could run out of insurance to protect directors.

Having entity claims outside the basic policy limit or as a separate limit protects the bank from using up the coverage. Alternately, the bank can purchase higher limits of coverage.

Side A, B, and C

Some D&O policies break up the coverage into three traditional coverage sections: A, B, and C.

Side A is coverage for individual directors and officers for claims where indemnification by the bank is not allowed by law or because the entity has no assets. Derivative suits are also covered here—suits by the bank against the directors.

Side B pays for incidents where individual directors and officers are sued when indemnification of the individuals is allowed. These are by far the most common claims.

Side C is coverage for the company (a.k.a. the bank). Some policies use the term "entity" to describe who is insured by this section.

★ Excess or Dedicated Side A Coverage

As has been said, directors' and officers' insurance covers a great deal of territory. All the bells and whistles, however, can draw coverage away from the primary purpose of the policy—protection of the directors and the officers.

The addition of separate, inviolate coverage just for claims that cannot be indemnified (so-called side A) can be a last ditch "stronghold" of coverage for D&Os.

Think of this as the "panic room" of bank insurance protection. A director is in legal trouble. For whatever reason, the bank cannot indemnify him or her. Dedicated side A protection is there, untouched by other bank claims.

The above scenario is the bleakest. When things are that bad, I'm not sure any amount of insurance is enough. Many banks are unwilling to offer such coverage, as it takes premium from other, perhaps more pressing, insurance needs.

Positions Covered by D&O

All policies define the term "insured persons." The contract may indicate directors, officers, employees, or some variation. Most contracts extend coverage to "past, present, and future" directors, officers, and employees.

Defense Within Limit

It is common for D&O policies to include the cost of defending a claim (attorneys' fees, etc.) within the policy limit of liability. That means that the amount of coverage purchased must be enough to cover the awards and defense costs of all claims. This can also be an issue to consider relative to aggregate limits.

When you buy $1 million of auto insurance, you get defense costs plus the $1 million. In D&O (most often), a $550K lawyer bill depletes the coverage available to pay the court-ordered award.

★ Duty to Defend

When there is a claim, who is responsible for the defense of the claim, the insurer or the insured? Who determines which attorney is used? Most common is a duty to defend by the insured, allowing the bank to choose defense counsel (usually with the approval of the insurer).

★ Common D&O Exclusions

The variety of D&O policies means that the unique exclusions number in the hundreds. Here are the most common:

- undue personal gain or profit

- intentional wrongful acts

- fraudulent, dishonest, or criminal acts

- bodily injury, property damage, or personal injury

- invasion of privacy

- ERISA claims

- employment practices liability

- lender liability

- trust activities

- nuclear reactions and contamination

- terrorism

- construction defect claims

- pollution

- acts while working as an officer or director of an outside entity

- failure to buy adequate insurance

- claims made by one insured against another insured

Some of the above exclusions exist because other policies provide better protection (as in the exclusion of bodily injury, where coverage is provided under a general liability policy). Other exclusions exist so that only insurance buyers with that exposure will buy the additional coverage. Why include trust liability coverage for all banks when only some have trust exposures?

★ Insured vs. Insured Exclusion

This exclusion prevents coverage when one director sues another director. If this exclusion is present, coverage should exist for past directors sued by current directors. There should also be coverage for actions brought against the board by bankruptcy trustees as well as coverage for actions brought against the board by a "whistleblower."

★ Regulatory Exclusion

Regulators may sue directors of troubled banks. A regulatory exclusion removes coverage for such actions. Accepting a D&O policy with a regulatory exclusion should be a desperate move, accepted only when there are no other options available in the marketplace. Ask your insurance advisor if there is a regulatory exclusion in your policy.

Hammer Clause

This appropriately named policy provision limits the insurer's liability should the insured refuse to accept a settlement offer from the plaintiff. In many cases, the insurance policy limits the insurer's obligation to the amount of the settlement offered. Some also restrict defense costs when the insured wishes to continue the fight.

Marital Estates Extension

The marital estates extension is now common in most D&O policies. It provides protection for the spouse of an "insured person" when a suit is brought against community property or property held jointly. Coverage only applies when the actions of the "insured person" cause the claim. For example, an officer is sued over issues surrounding a loan application. The officer's spouse is also brought into the suit, as he or she owns the family home. The marital estates extension provides the spouse with coverage.

★ Non-Cancellation Endorsement

Who can cancel your policy? Can the insurance company decide it no longer wants to provide coverage? Too often, I see policies with terms that allow the insurer to bail out with sixty days' notice. Look for your insurer to provide coverage through the full policy term. Get the cancellation clause adjusted to prevent midterm cancellation—other than for nonpayment of premium.

Note: Most policies do not guarantee premiums. An insurer may not be able to cancel your policy, but it may be able to triple your premiums!

★ Multiyear Policies

Unlike most business insurance contracts, many D&O policies are issued with two- or three-year terms. Depending on competition or the current condition of the insurance market, insurers may offer discounts for prepaying premiums for multiyear policies.

While the policy may be issued for three years, insurers often have policy provisions that allow for premiums to be adjusted if circumstances at the bank deteriorate or if there have been claims.

Multiyear policy coverage limits are stated for a single year. Aggregate limits are annually reinstated. A $1 million claim in year one does not reduce the coverage available in year three.

Nonprofit Service

It is quite common for community bank officers to serve on boards of directors for nonprofit organizations. Nonprofit service coverage provides protection for actions by an "insured person" arising out of his or her work as a board member for a nonprofit when it is considered part of his or her bank duties to perform such a public service. Coverage is usually in excess over any insurance or assets the nonprofit has.

Frankly, this coverage is nothing to crow about. For coverage to apply, the nonprofit has to exhaust its assets and insurance. Having coverage on the bank's D&O is certainly better than nothing. However, the insurers are not giving away much here.

★ Civil Money Penalties

Look at the definition of "loss" in your D&O policy. You will find that fines and penalties are not included in the coverage. The FDIC does not care. Neither do your state regulators.

Civil money penalties (CMP) insurance is a part of many D&O policies. It provides coverage for penalties assessed by regulatory agencies against directors and officers. The bank itself is not eligible for coverage.

Some insurers require that the individual directors who want CMP pay for the coverage with a personal check. Others allow the bank to pay the premiums as long as the bank certifies that the directors have paid the bank for the protection.

Premiums for CMP for community banks are almost always under $100 per director per year for $100K of coverage.

There is currently a fair amount of discussion about this issue. Supposedly, the FDIC is concerned that buying civil money damages coverage could cause problems.

Here is what an underwriter recently told me: "We are getting lots of questions on this from our community bank agents on how to advise their clients on whether or not to purchase this coverage. (Our) position is that this has been the long-standing position of the industry to make D&O civil money penalties coverage available to our clients. We believe that there continues to be a reasonable basis under the law to support the permissibility of this coverage. We want to remind our clients that (we are) not in a position to provide insureds with legal advice. The client will have to make a determination for themselves, in consultation with their own legal counsel on whether to purchase or retain this coverage[*sic*]."

Good advice. Talk with your bank's attorney.

I counsel against buying CMP coverage. I think it goes contrary to the expressed desires of the regulators. We may not like it. However, regulators have made no secret of their interpretation of the regulations on this issue.

Employment-Related Practices Coverage

Employment practices liability coverage can be a part of the D&O insurance or a separate policy. The protection provided includes such issues as wrongful discharge, harassment, discrimination, etc. Check the policy's definition of "wrongful employment act." Does it include only certain acts, such as sexual harassment? Or is the coverage broad, including workplace harassment, for example? Are discrimination suits brought by third parties covered? Remember that including employment practices claims in your organization's D&O policy could affect the limit of liability available for other claims. Negotiate your coverage so that claims paid for employment practices suits are outside the limits of coverage for your entity and directors' and officers'.

See the separate discussion on employment practices liability policies.

Bankers' Professional Liability Insurance

Some insurers use a separate coverage section of the D&O policy called Bankers' Professional Liability (BPL). Coverage is provided for a broad range of financial services, including:

    depository services
    insurance services
    notary services
    investment and brokerage services
    certain real estate services
    general banking services

electronic data processing services
escrow services
estate planning
loan servicing
serving of lock boxes
tax planning
administration of credit cards

Lender's liability claims are often included in a separate coverage section. Some insurers will exclude insurance sales and brokerage operations in their basic policies. Coverage can be added back by endorsement.

Trust operations are also commonly excluded. Banks that need protection for such operations can have coverage added for an additional premium. See the separate section on trust errors and omissions insurance.

Be aware of policies that provide only coverage for professional liability suits brought by customers. Many causes of legal action can come from third parties—spouses, beneficiaries, the vendors, customers, or contractors of your customer. Regulators may bring suit, as may other financial institutions that participate in loan packages with your bank.

Some policies require that the relationship between the bank and the party bringing suit be based on a fee relationship. Review the policy to be certain that insurers use a broad definition of professional services to include any transaction where the bank receives some tangible benefit, rather than a narrow requirement that there be a direct monetary relationship.

Here are exclusions that are common to bankers' professional liability insurance:

- pollution liability
- construction defect claims
- investment banking activities
- fee and commission disputes
- bodily injury and property damage
- personal injury

★ Fiduciary Liability

Several years ago, I was meeting with the president of a small bank and the head of the human resources department. I'd been hired a few weeks earlier to perform a due diligence review of the bank's insurance, and we were going through a list of concerns I had identified in my analysis.

"Your ERISA exposure is not covered," I said. The HR VP laughed. A few minutes later, she was not laughing.

The Employee Retirement and Income Security Act (ERISA) is the federal law passed in 1974 that governs employee benefit plans. Most people know it for its impact on pension plans. It also makes administrators of employee benefit plans *personally* liable for errors and mistakes. The act covers pension plans, group health insurance, disability coverage, dental, and any other employee benefit program an employer offers—what ERISA calls "welfare plans."

It was the "personally liable" part that got the HR manager's attention. "Explain what you mean by personally liable," she said.

The issue is pretty straightforward. If you administer a health insurance or pension plan, you are liable for any mistakes you make—you, not your company, is liable. If you forget to add an employee to the health insurance, it's your house and bank account that is tapped to pay a claim. If the premium doesn't get sent and the policy is cancelled, it's your assets on the line. Fail to make decisions in a prudent manner about the 401(k) plan, and guess what happens to your savings account.

The HR manager had even more to be upset about when I mentioned the next kicker. In addition to personal liability, ERISA specifically forbids indemnification by the administrator's employer. If you make a mistake, your company cannot bail you out. Insurance is the only third-party solution to the personal liability provision.

The Fiduciary section to the D&O policy (or a separate policy) is the solution to the ERISA problem. The coverage provides protection for "wrongful acts" that result in a claim against the administrator of benefit plans. Premiums range from a few hundred dollars to thousands of dollars, depending on the size of the employer.

We are not talking about errors to customer accounts here. Fiduciary liability provides coverage for errors in administering your bank's employee benefit plan.

By the way, many people confuse ERISA fiduciary liability with the ERISA bond requirement. The law mandates that employee pension and retirement plans have a bond of 10 percent of the assets (up to $500K) to cover loss of the funds through embezzlement. Some fiduciary policies include the fidelity coverage. Most do not. For most banks, your financial institution bond provides an extension of coverage for the ERISA bond requirement.

Some businesses and insurance agents confuse employee benefit liability insurance with the FRIP. Bad call! The FRIP covers errors and omissions in the administration of benefit plans. The employee benefit liability policy covers mistakes but excludes ERISA liabilities. The wrong claim against an employer with employee benefit liability could result in a "for sale" sign going up in front of the HR manager's house.

IRA/Keogh/Welfare and Retirement Plan Liability

This coverage section provides coverage for the bank against liability caused by errors or omissions while acting as administrator or trustee of IRA or HR 10/Keogh plans for others.

Here are some of the issues that come from such plans:

errors in overall administration

failure to add employees

removing employees improperly

imprudent advice

failure to follow laws and regulations

Lender Liability

Lender liability insurance protects the financial institution against lawsuits alleging improper procedures, extension of credit, refusal to lend, or improper servicing of loans. The exposure is often excluded in the professional liability section of the D&O policy and then added back at an additional premium. Limits of coverage and deductibles may be separately applied as well.

Every directors' and officers' liability policy is unique. Read your policy!

Securities Liability

Securities liability provides protection for the entity against lawsuits resulting from the purchase, sale, or offer to purchase or sell any securities issued by the insured (sale of the bank's own stock).

While not a lot of explanation is needed to describe this coverage, stockholder actions against board members are the most frequent area of D&O claims for publicly traded banks.

Trust Errors & Omissions

Trust E&O coverage protects the bank from liability arising out of wrongful acts in the administration of trust accounts. The coverage may be an endorsement to the D&O policy or a separate, stand-alone policy. In any event, make sure that coverage for this protection does not erode the aggregate limit of coverage on the D&O. If you offer trust services, your trust E&O coverage should be a separate limit of coverage.

★ Electronic Banking Liability

Some insurers provide this coverage in the D&O policy. Some make it a separate policy. See the chapter dedicated to this important protection.

Chapter Seventeen: ★ Independent Director's Liability Insurance

Several insurance companies are now discussing selling coverage directly to independent board members to provide coverage when the corporate D&O doesn't respond due to government intervention, bankruptcy, or insolvency. Hartford Financial Services Group, Inc. offers a policy called "Priority Protection-IDL." Chubb Specialty Insurance calls its product "Personal Director's Liability Insurance."

Here are the issues to consider if you are going to buy your own D&O insurance:

– What are the policy limits?

– Is there a retention/deductible?

– In what circumstances will the policy pay? Must the corporate directors' and officers' policy respond first?

– Who selects the defense team—you or the insurer?

– Is coverage included for actions brought against a non-director spouse?

– Assuming the policy is a claims-made, what are the extended reporting provisions available if I cancel it?

Chapter Eighteen: Employment Practices Liability Insurance

An employee claims to have been harassed by a supervisor. A teller who was discharged for chronic customer service complaints claims age discrimination. An unsuccessful job applicant alleges he didn't get the job because of his race. These are all liabilities included in employment-related practices insurance. The topic was touched on briefly in the D&O section, since coverage can be included in that policy. We'll go into more detail here.

Summary of Coverage
The policy is designed to address liabilities that come out of the employment relationship. Workers' compensation, issues involving unemployment insurance, and ERISA are excluded.

Coverage is generally included for harassment, discrimination, wrongful discharge, failure to hire, and failure to promote.

No Standardized Coverage Forms

As there are no standard EPLI policies, each insurer's policy and proposal must be evaluated on its own merits.

If you have been reading along, you should have realized that this is a constant theme in bank specialty insurance policies. A detailed analysis of the coverage is necessary. Any time you get alternative proposals, each policy must be reviewed in detail.

Claims-Made Policy

See tchapter fifteen for a complete discussion describing claims-made policy issues.

Limit of Coverage

Most EPLI policies have a limit per occurrence and a policy limit of coverage for the total of all claims, called an aggregate limit. As claims are paid, you use up the limit of coverage available for future claims.

Defense Within Limit

The cost of defending an employment-related claim (attorneys' fees, etc.) will eat up your limit of coverage. When looking for the correct limit of coverage, consider the cost of the legal system in your calculations.

★ Definition of Wrongful Employment Practice

Each EPLI policy will contain a definition of the wrongful acts that are included in the policy.

Here are some acts to be considered when reviewing coverage:

- discrimination
- negligent hiring
- wrongful discharge, evaluation, discipline, or promotion

- employment-related personal injury (libel or slander)

- sexual harassment

- workplace harassment

- failure to hire

- wrongful termination

- wrongful retention

- wrongful infliction of emotional distress

- excessive or wrongful discipline

- retaliation

If an act is outside the definition of wrongful act, there is no coverage.

Definition of Harassment

Some policies narrowly define this coverage as "sexual harassment." A better (broader) definition is "workplace harassment" or "harassment including sexual harassment." That small change makes a huge difference in protection.

★ Common Exclusions

Here are some of the more common exclusions in the employment practices liability insurance policy:

ERISA, workers' compensation, and disability benefits

Fair Labor Standards Act claims (wage/hour issues)

unemployment insurance benefits

lockouts, strikes, and replacement workers

severance pay or vacation time owed

medical, dental, and life insurance benefits

★ Third-Party Harassment Liability

Most insurers now expand the employment practices liability insurance coverage to harassment of third parties—suppliers, customers, and contractors.

Here is the definition used by one insurer:

Third-party harassment act means any actual or alleged:

1. violation of any federal, state, provincial, or local statutory law, common law, or civil law prohibiting discrimination of any kind;

2. harassment, including any type of sexual, religious, racial, sexual orientation, pregnancy, disability, age, or national origin-based harassment;

3. defamation, libel, slander, disparagement, or invasion of privacy;

4. false arrest, false imprisonment, or malicious persecution; or

5. bullying of a natural person other than an employee, officer, or director and other than as a part of a lending act.

I almost always suggest this coverage even though there are some overlaps with the personal injury section of the commercial general liability policy.

★ Fair Labor Standards and Wage/Hour Claims

The federal law known as the Fair Labor Standards Act (FLSA) establishes minimum wages, overtime pay, child labor, hours worked standards, and record-keeping requirements. Legal actions brought against employers are almost always excluded by employment practices liability coverage. However, insurers are sometimes open to offering coverage for defense costs at some relatively small amounts; $100K is common. Ask your insurance advisor.

★ Duty to Defend

Does the insurance company defend you in a claim, or do you pick the attorney? Most banks will want to control this aspect of a lawsuit—placing the duty to defend on the insured. Your insurer will probably have the right to veto your choice.

Special Insurance Company Provisions

Some employment practices liability insurance policies include special features for policyholders. Usually these are measures to prevent losses. Insurers may provide a human resources "hot line," allowing free access to experts to discuss employment actions and situations. Such gives the bank information and opinions on issues that could lead to a claim.

Some insurers will reduce the applicable deductible if a claim results from an action where the insured called an attorney prior to the termination of an employee. Some insurers allow you to call your own lawyer. Others require that you use their attorney.

Chapter Nineteen: Financial Institutions Fraud-Bond

The financial institutions bond (also called the bankers' bond or the bankers' blanket bond) protects the bank for issues of dishonesty and fraud. Claims include: employee theft, robbery, loan fraud, kidnapping, wire transfer fraud, counterfeit currency, and computer systems fraud.

The bond is a first-party policy; it protects the bank against loss of the bank's assets.

Employee Dishonesty/Fidelity

The employee dishonesty section is often called "Coverage A," as it was designated as such in the original "Form 24" bond used in the early part of the 1900s. Coverage is provided for dishonest or fraudulent acts committed by employees acting alone or in collusion with others—such as embezzlement.

The original bond form required that the employee intended to cause the bank a loss or to obtain some financial benefit. Such wording excluded "Robin Hood" events where the employee steals to benefit another person. Current forms broaden out coverage to include gains to others. Coverage is triggered by an intentional loss to the bank caused by an employee who is attempting to benefit himself or herself, or someone else.

On Premises

Robbery, burglary, and mysterious disappearances are all covered by this section of the bond. The property stolen can be owned by the bank, a customer, or an employee.

Property is broadly defined by most policies to include money, certificated securities, negotiable instruments, certificates of deposit, documents of title, evidences of debt, security agreements, withdrawal orders, certificates of origin or title, letters of credit, insurance policies, abstracts of title, deeds and mortgages on real estate, revenue and other stamps, tokens, unsold state lottery tickets, books of account and other records stored on tangible media, gems, jewelry, precious metals in any form, and other tangible personal property.

In Transit

This section provides coverage for loss of property resulting directly from robbery, larceny, theft, or misplacement while the property is in transit away from the bank. Property must be in the custody of either a person acting as a messenger of the bank or a transportation company.

Money, gems, jewelry, or precious metals being transported by a transportation company must be in an armored vehicle. Money transported by a courier (not in an armored car) is not covered.

Money being transported by a bank employee is usually covered, even if the transportation is made by private car.

Counterfeit Currency

Coverage is included in this section for loss resulting from the good faith receipt by the bank of counterfeit money. Be sure the definition of "currency" or "money" includes currencies of foreign governments.

Agents Coverage

Amends the policy definition of "employee" to include persons, partnerships, or corporations (such as conveyancers or collectors of rents or savings from persons making systematic deposits with the insured, and excluding servicing contractors, managers of real property, data processing organizations, and independent software contractors), duly elected or appointed by the bank to serve as an agent.

Audit and Claims Expense

Covers expenses for audits or examinations required by state or federal regulators when the audits are conducted either by such authorities or by independent accountants due to the discovery of a loss under employee dishonesty/fidelity coverage.

Automated Teller Machines

Loss of property located within an ATM machine, including damage to the machine itself, caused by burglary, robbery, or attempted burglary or robbery. Some policies limit coverage to ATMs that are a part of a bank building. Beware of wording that requires that the ATM be "permanent."

Check Kiting Fraud

Covers loss resulting directly from checks that are finally not paid because of a check kiting fraud established against the bank.

Computer Systems Fraud

Covers loss from a fraudulent entry or a change of electronic data or computer program within a covered computer system. Coverage only applies when money/property is transferred, paid, or delivered when an account of either the insured or a customer is debited or credited, or when an unauthorized or fictitious account is debited or credited.

Claim examples:

A computer hacker accesses a bank customer's account and moves money to his or her personal account.

Software is maliciously installed on the bank's computer system, which systematically moves funds to an offshore bank account.

Data Processing Service Operations

Consider this coverage if your bank provides data processing services to other financial institutions. Coverage is for losses sustained by a customer of the bank, resulting directly from a fraudulent entry of electronic data or change of electronic data within the insured's computer system.

Debit Card Coverage

Provides coverage for losses resulting directly from the fraudulent use of a debit card to obtain cash or pay for products or services by gaining access to an electronic payment device, provided that such device, as part of the transaction, electronically verifies the customer's available funds in the customer's depository account at the insured's bank.

Watch for limitations of coverage for events originating outside the United States.

Destruction of Data or Programs by Hacker

Covers loss resulting directly from the malicious destruction of, or damage to, computer programs owned by the bank, or for which the bank is legally liable, while stored within a computer system.

Protection is usually included for the cost of duplicating damaged or destroyed data or computer programs from backup sources.

If the computer programs cannot be duplicated from a backup, the insurance company will pay the additional costs to restore damaged or destroyed data.

Destruction of Data or Programs by Virus

Covers loss from the malicious destruction of, or damage to, electronic or computer programs owned by the bank, or for which the bank is legally liable, while stored within a computer system. Protection is usually included for the cost of duplicating damaged or destroyed data or computer programs from backup sources, or the additional costs of restoring the damaged data.

Forgery/Unauthorized Signature

Provides protection against a loss caused by an unauthorized signature or the alteration of a negotiable instrument, including a counterfeit check, letter of acceptance, withdrawal order, certificate of deposit, letter of credit, or receipt of the withdrawal of property. This coverage usually does not apply to an evidence of debt.

Fraudulent Mortgages

Covers loss through the bank having, in good faith, acted upon any real property mortgages or similar instruments that prove to be defective by reason of the signature on such instruments having been obtained by trick or false pretenses.

Indemnity for Injury or Death of Directors or Employees

Covers payments made to directors or employees who were injured or whose death was caused by any person who was committing or attempting to commit any act of larceny, theft, robbery, or burglary.

Kidnap-Ransom-Extortion

Covers the loss of money surrendered and expenses incurred as a result of:

- the actual or alleged kidnapping of an insured person

- a threat to kill, injure, or kidnap an insured person

- a threat to cause damage to and/or contaminate or pollute the insured's property

- a threat to disseminate, divulge, or utilize any confidential, private, or secret information unique to the insured's business, which is protected by physical or electronic controls

- ; or

- a threat to alter, adulterate, or destroy any of the insured's computer programs by introducing instructions or data that are not authorized by the insured into the insured's computer systems.

Some policy forms fail to adequately provide coverage for either e-commerce extortion or extortion that includes the threat of releasing private information.

Safe Depository

Some insurers provide coverage for a safe depository as a separate policy. Others include it in the bond. The coverage provides for all sums the bank is legally liable to pay because of the loss, damage, or destruction of a customer's property from a safe depository—loss by theft, fire, windstorm, or virtually any other cause. Some policies allow for the exclusion of money at a reduced premium.

Safe depository coverage can be written in two broad ways:

Liability of Depository – covers loss that the insured is legally obligated to pay by reason of liability for loss of a customers' property. This form of protection gives the bank coverage for its liability. There would be no coverage for destruction caused by a lightning strike, for example, unless an attorney found a judge that ruled the bank responsible for lighting.

Loss of Customers' Property – covers loss of customers' property by burglary or robbery, or any attempt thereat, or for damage to or destruction of customers' property, regardless of the liability of the bank. This coverage is quite broad and more expensive.

Determining the limits of safe depository coverage that your bank needs is a tough call. What is the largest exposure to loss you have at any of your locations? What do your customers have stored in their boxes? Both are unanswerable questions. Start at $1 million and get quotes for more.

Securities Fraud/Forgery

Covers losses resulting from extending credit on the faith of stock certificates, documents of title, deeds, mortgages, certificates of title, corporate or personal guarantees, evidences of debt, and security agreements that are forged, altered, counterfeited, lost, or stolen. The bank must have relied in good faith upon an original instrument. The document must have been in the physical possession of the bank, its correspondent, or representative.

Servicing Contractors

Extends coverage for loss resulting from the dishonest acts of a person or organization that collects and records payments on real estate mortgage, home improvement loans, or a manager of real property under the control of the insured.

Stop Payment or Wrongful Dishonor

Provides coverage for loss that the insured is legally liable to pay due to the insured's:

- failure to comply with a customer's request to stop payment on a negotiable instrument
- refusing to pay a negotiable instrument
- , or
- failure to give proper notice of dishonor.

Telefacsimile Transfer Fraud

Covers loss resulting directly from the bank having, in good faith, transferred or delivered funds, certificated securities, or uncertificated securities through a computer system covered under the terms of the computer systems fraud coverage section, in reliance upon a fraudulent instruction received through a telefacsimile device.

Some insurers have "callback" requirements that exclude coverage when a confirmation phone call is not made for transfers over a certain limit. Negotiate the callback limit to match your operations.

Trading Loss
The employee dishonesty coverage in many bonds excludes losses involving trading (any purchase, exchange, or sale transaction). Trading loss coverage buys back the exclusion, providing coverage for a loss caused by an employee's fraudulent trades.

Transit Cash Letter Rider
Cash letters are usually covered within the "in transit" coverage. Some insurers offer coverage that extends the protection by eliminating the deductible, providing reimbursement for reproduction costs, and extending coverage beyond the final destination of the cash letter to the financial institution upon which an item was drawn. Insurers usually require that the front and back of each item placed in the cash letter be photocopied.

Voice-Initiated Transfer Fraud
This coverage is available only in conjunction with computer systems fraud coverage. It provides the bank with protection against loss resulting directly from the insured having, in good faith, transferred funds from a customer's account through a computer system covered under the terms of the computer systems fraud section, in reliance upon a fraudulent voice instruction transmitted by telephone.

Be cautious of "callback" requirements that exclude coverage when a confirmation phone call is not made for transfers over a certain limit. Negotiate the call-back limit to match your operations.

Voice Computer System Fraud

Covers loss resulting directly from toll call charges incurred due to the fraudulent use or fraudulent manipulation of an account code or systems password required to obtain access to the insured's voice computer system.

Be aware of callback provisions in your coverage.

★ Multiyear Policies

As with directors' and officers' insurance, most bank bonds can be issued with two- or three-year terms. Depending on competition or on the current condition of the insurance market, insurers may offer discounts for prepaying premiums for multiyear policies.

While the poli

cy may be issued for three years, insurers often have policy provisions that allow for premiums to be adjusted if circumstances at the bank deteriorate or if claims have been made.

★ Non-Cancellation Endorsement

Who can cancel your bond? What if you have several claims and your insurer no longer wants to provide coverage? Several insurers have sixty days notice of cancellation as standard. Insist that your insurer provide coverage through the full policy term. Get the cancellation clause adjusted to prevent midterm cancellation—other than for nonpayment of premium.

★ Dishonest Acts by Dishonest Employees

Almost all bank bonds I review include a clause that excludes claims of embezzlement when the employee is known to have committed a past dishonest act.

The example I regularly use is of a fifty-five-year-old teller who, when she was seventeen, stole a car.

In my example, I say that the woman has been a good employee for fifteen years. One day, in a conversation with a bank officer, the employee reveals her youthful indiscretion. Nothing really unusual, just two adults talking about their past. The officer goes on her way, noting how the teller has turned her life around.

Two years later, our "trusted" teller is found to have stolen $200K from the bank.

Won't you be surprised to learn that your bond excludes coverage, as 95 percent of bonds do?

The standard language in most bond forms excludes coverage for an employee who is known by a bank officer to have committed a past "dishonest act."

Further, most bonds do not define the term "dishonest act."

Is coverage excluded for an employee who has "stolen" a pad of paper? How about an employee who has made personal phone calls or surfed ESPN.com during working hours?

Your insurance may not give you guidance.

Most would agree that each of these events is dishonest. How about telling a lie about being sick? How about being unfaithful to a spouse? How about an exaggerated claim on an employment application?

Some insurers put a dollar value on their exclusion so that coverage is only affected if the value of the dishonest act is more than $5K and has a relationship to the individual's employment.

That, I think, makes sense. The current, broad exclusion is needlessly restrictive, going well beyond the intent of most insurers.

If you cannot get your insurer to define dishonesty, be sure your officers understand the restrictions of coverage. Anyone who becomes aware of an employee's past dishonesty should report the facts to an appropriate person at the bank. You can then put your insurer on notice so that waivers can be put into place.

Draft a letter that can be sent annually to bank officers, reminding them of the bond policy clause. Better yet, get your insurer to define "dishonest act."

★ Employee Theft Claims Involving Loans

It is almost standard now for bank bonds to exclude coverage for an employee dishonesty loss involving a loan when the employee was not in collusion with another person. In other words, if the employee theft involves a loan, your employee cannot be acting alone.

While I have often tried, I have been unable to get an insurer to soften this language at all.

Further, most bonds exclude coverage for employee theft claims involving a loan when the employee did not expect to share in the proceeds of the loss. So-called "Robin Hood" claims involving a loan would not be covered.

Chapter Twenty: E-Banking Risk Liability Coverage

The first edition of this book included a dismissal of many of the coverage provisions and the general format of the e-banking insurance policies in place at the time.

In fact, the e-banking section of the book began, "I am not a big fan of the current crop of e-banking insurance policies. While these policies have their place, I question the value of the insurance contracts for most community banks, given the breadth of coverage available in the bond, directors' and officers', and package policies."

Over the past two years, my opinion of e-banking insurance has changed. It is now a vital part of a bank insurance program. Insurers have built the policies to mesh with the bond and directors' and officers' insurance. Exclusions and coverage limitations have been added to the basic bank policies, making e-banking insurance a necessity. Buy it. If you don't have it, buy it now.

Suppose that your computer system is hacked and private data is breached. Customer information is in the hands of the bad guys. Lawsuits will be filed based on your failure to protect customer privacy, breach of duty, and lost business opportunities.

This chapter is concerned with liability claims that come from computer systems, Internet banking, and electronic commerce.

First, recall that your financial institution bond provides coverage for your loss of money due to computer theft and fraud losses. (See chapter nineteen.)

The "injuries" to third parties and subsequent legal actions triggered by Internet and computer use are the realm of e-banking liability insurance (EBLI).

As with most bank specialty insurance policies, EBLI policies are unique to each insurance carrier and must be studied carefully. The following are some common coverage sections and considerations.

Loss Event Liability

The basic policy includes coverage for liability that arises out of any unauthorized use of, or unauthorized access to, electronic data or software within your covered electronic business systems. Coverage is also usually included for liability claims of spreading a virus or malicious code, computer theft, extortion, or any unintentional act, mistake, error, or omission made by your employees or your subcontractors in the course of their duties for your bank.

Policy Aggregate

Most policies include a limit per claim and an aggregate limit that caps your total coverage for the combination of all claims.

Business Income Loss

In the event that your e-banking system goes down, you may (so the theory goes) lose income or incur extra expenses in advertising. This section provides coverage for such losses.

Dependent Business

Provides loss of business income protection for the loss of services provided to you by others for Web services, e-banking support, and the like.

Intellectual Property

Indemnifies the bank from the liability caused by the inappropriate use of the intellectual property of others on a Web site or e-banking facility. Can include copyright infringement, theft of ideas, and trademark misuse.

Public Relations Expenses

Provides payment for the use of public relations firms and advertising to mitigate the damage to public perception should an e-banking breach occur. (Note: Your bank faces enormous risks for events that cause a loss of reputation. Public relations expense coverage in your e-banking liability insurance funds a relatively minor part of your overall reputation risk exposures. How's your risk management plan?)

★ Privacy Breach Remediation Expenses

A hacker gets into your computer system. Private customer data is released. Your bank's e-banking insurance will/should provide coverage for lawsuits that come from the breach. How about the expenses of informing customers of the breach and providing credit tracking services?

Simply put, there is usually no coverage in most bond, D&O, or e-banking insurance policies for these expenses. Some insurers add coverage by endorsement (and separate charge). Some offer coverage within the package policy (Chubb and OneBeacon, namely). I have seen coverage endorsed to the bond and to the D&O policy. Talk with your insurance advisor to see how your insurance responds to these issues.

Chapter Twenty-One: ★ Terrorism Insurance

In the days before September 11, 2001, nobody (well, few of us) thought about terrorism. After the events of that day, this consideration became a very big deal.

Your insurance starts off (except for workers' compensation) excluding losses caused by terrorism. If you want the coverage, you pay an extra premium for protection to be added.

Insurers now offer coverage in conjunction with the Terrorism Risk Insurance Act (TRIA), which provides protection for terrorist acts that fall within certain parameters. The federal law was initiated in 2002, extended in 2005, extended again in 2007, and now is scheduled to run through 2014.

Here is some general information about TRIA:

– TRIA is a federal program with mandatory insurance company participation.

– It covers foreign or domestic terrorism attacks on US property that cause at least $5 million in damages.

- Reinsurance starts when total insured losses hit $100 million.

- The feds pay for 85 percent of any losses above an insurance company's deductible.

- The insurer of record is responsible for 15 percent of any losses after a 20 percent deductible.

- Annual losses covered by the program are capped at $100 billion.

Some states require that insurance companies provide full terrorism coverage. Some states allow insurers to exclude acts of terrorism unless the insured pays an additional premium.

According to TRIA, to be certified as an act of terrorism:

- An event must be an act of terrorism.

- The event must be violent and dangerous to human life, property, or infrastructure.

- The act must cause damage either within the United States or, if outside the United States, to an air carrier or vessel or on the premises of a United States mission.

- The intent of the act must be to coerce the US population or affect the conduct of the government of the United States.

- If an act takes place and it is related to a war declared by Congress, the act may be certified for only workers' compensation coverage. Further, no action is certified if the commercial property and casualty aggregate losses are less than $5 million.

Therefore, a "small-scale" terrorist attack (under $5 million in damage or not qualified as certifiable) is covered by your insurance program—with or without the purchase of TRIA coverage. If you decline TRIA coverage, you have no coverage for a "certified event."

Insurers offer TRIA quotes at policy inception and renewal. The exception is workers' compensation, where TRIA coverage is automatically included and cannot be removed.

I suggest that banks ask their insurance advisors to explain the full impact of a decision not to buy terrorism insurance.

Chapter Twenty-Two: Your Insurance Renewal

It is almost an automatic part of the insurance transaction for most community banks: the renewal.

Each year, your agent comes to you (usually just before your insurance expires) with the premiums for the next policy term. If your agent delivers a renewal premium that stays the same as you pay now, you're happy. If the premium goes up 5 percent, well, that's the way of life, isn't it? If the premium goes up by 15 percent, your agent tells you that prices in insurance are going up, and there is nothing to be done. You realize you have little time, and the current coverages renew in a few weeks.

Is money being left on the table? Is your insurance company providing you with the best coverage at their best price? If your premium drops by 5 percent, how do you know that it shouldn't have dropped by 15 percent?

There are complications. Some banks want to deal with a specific agent in town, usually a customer or board member. Perhaps you wish to use two agents or more. I have bank clients who own their insurance agent. I have bank clients whose agent is their brother. I was recently told of a bank where the CEO's wife was the bank's insurance agent.

It is tough to bid your insurance when your agent is family.

Here are some broad principles I have developed over my years of working with banks on the renewal of their insurance:

- The most important part of the insurance transaction is the relationship the insurance buyer has with the insurance agent. That being said, few agents have unique skills and resources. Almost any insurance buyer can easily find an agent who will provide superior service. In fact, a search will usually uncover several.

- Insurance agents all tout the exceptional service they provide. The reality is often different.

- A match in personalities between the insurance agent and the insurance buyer is important.

- Trust between the agent and the insurance buyer is important.

- The geographic location of an agent is important. Different states have different laws. Regional insurance markets are different. Understanding the insurer's resources in an area can help at the time of a claim.

- An agent's specific industry expertise can trump the importance of an agent's location.

- An insurance agent's access to a broad range of insurance companies is important.

- An insurance agent's relationship with the insurance companies is important. Large premium volume with an insurer means that the agent has some pull with them—in both underwriting and claims.

- When using multiple insurance agents in a bid process, the buyer must assign insurers to agents. Insurers will not release quotes to multiple agents. You either assign insurance companies to specific participating agents, or chaos will ensue. The assignment of a company to a particular agent is important. An insurer's performance for a particular insured does vary (in coverage, service, and price) depending on the agent who has brought in the business.

– Insurance underwriters have wide latitude in the premiums they can charge and the coverage they can offer. Underwriters are charged with finding the right price based on the perception of the risk and the appetite of the insurance company. Most insurance rating starts with some kind of base premium. Underwriters can then increase premiums by as much as 30 percent. They can also decrease premiums as much as 30 percent from the base. (Note to insurance people: Yes, I am overly simplifying the rating process. However, the fact remains that underwriters can largely do whatever they want with premiums.) The authority of underwriting managers and supervisors is even greater.

– Underwriters can almost always hit a stationary price target if they like your bank, respect the agent, and want your business. Tell the underwriter that he will lose the account unless he can meet or beat a competitor's price, and he will beat the price. Give him a last shot, and that shot will almost always hit the target.

– The threat of losing a bid or an account makes agents and insurers more sharp. Competition keeps service high, coverage broad, and pencils sharpened.

– Price is always an important consideration. It is rarely the only factor. This is as it should be.

– Underwriters have a great deal of latitude in coverages, too, though not as broad as with pricing. However, when pushed for a reasonable coverage concession, most underwriters can get the job done—if they really want to.

– Most banks prefer to renew their policies with the same agent and same insurer. In most instances, where the relationship of the agent with the bank is stable, a premium savings of 20 percent is needed for the account to move to another agent.

– Without someone pushing the underwriter, renewal premiums will be delivered to the agent a week before the policies expire. This is intentional by the insurance company. It is either intentionally done so that the insured has few options, or it is done because the insurance company is not tuned in to what their clients need. Either one is not the way partners treat each other.

Chapter Twenty-Three: The Insurance Renewal Decision – Your Options

You can take only four paths in the renewal of your insurance policies:

– Renew your current policies with your current agent using your current insurer.

– Use your current agent to get quotes from multiple insurers.

– Agent selection. Interview several agents and pick the best.

– Review multiple agents. Pick several. Let them bid using multiple insurers.

Each approach has advantages and disadvantages:

Renew With Your Current Agent, Using Your Current Insurer

Advantages to You	Disadvantages to You
Easy on you, the insurance buyer, as your agent has all the information he needs. Shows loyalty to your agent and insurer.	No competitive pressures to push your agent or insurer to provide a better price and coverage. Coverage errors may exist. Nobody checks your agent's work. You may miss opportunities from viable insurers - better premium/better coverage. You're stuck with the premium and coverage your insurer throws at you.

Your Current Agent Obtains Quotes From Multiple Insurers

Advantages to You	Disadvantages to You
Easy on you, as your agent already has the information he needs. Competition pushes insurers to offer better pricing and better coverage. Shows loyalty to your agent.	No competitive pressures to push the agent to provide a better price and coverage. He knows he has your business Coverage errors made in the past may persist, as nobody is checking your current agent's work. You may miss quotes from viable insurers that your agent does not have access to or know about. Your relationship with your current insurer may suffer.

Agent Selection Process – You Interview Multiple Agents and Select the Best

Advantages fo You	Disadvantages to You
You're exposed to multiple agents and their ideas, yielding alternatives. Selected agent may be more aggressive to impress you, the new client. Competition pushes insurers to offer better pricing and better coverage.	Competition among insurers, but the agent is not pushed to perform. The process can involve a great deal of your time and effort as you gather information and educate the agents and insurers. You may miss quotes from viable insurers, as only one agent is marketing for you. Your relationship with your "old" agent may suffer if he is not selected.

Review Multiple Agents. Pick Several. Let Them Bid Using Multiple Insurers

Advantages to You	Disadvantages to You
Ultimate competitive pressures are exerted, as all participants must perform in order to win. Competition means the knives are out and the pencils are sharp. A wider range of competition can result in lowest prices and broadest coverages. You are exposed to multiple agents, their approaches, insurers, and ideas.	The process can involve a great deal of your time and effort. Comparing and evaluating the resulting bids may be difficult without help. Your relationship with your "old" agent may suffer if he is not selected. Your relationship with your "old" insurer may suffer if that insurer is not selected. You may have to start new relationships with agents and insurers.

133

The Decision Process

Here's a chart that outlines the overall thought process in deciding which approach to take with your upcoming renewal.

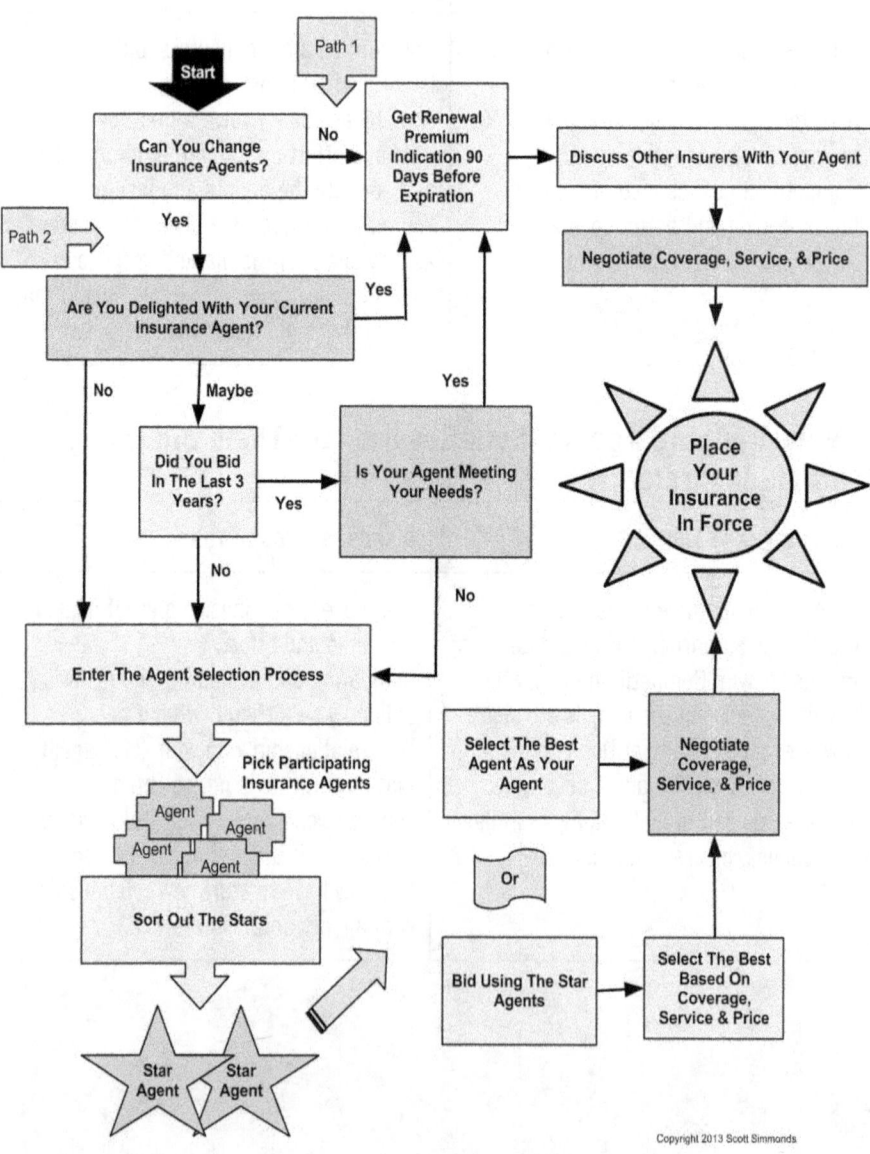

Copyright 2013 Scott Simmonds

Path One: You Can't Change Agents?

I mentioned before that my years of working with community banks have shown me that well over half cannot, for a variety of reasons, change insurance agents. Some banks have a subsidiary that sells insurance (tough not to buy your insurance from your own company). Some bank's insurance agent is a large depositor, stockholder, or board member.

Having close ties to your insurance agent can be a good thing. I've said earlier that the most important part of the insurance transaction is the agent's relationship with the insurance buyer. Close, almost family relationships can mean that your agent is in there swinging for you. There is, however, the danger that complacency can set in. Prevent that by setting high expectations for your agent.

If, by necessity or by decision, you are staying with your current insurance agent, start the renewal process early. Meet with your agent 120 days before your coverage expires. Push for a premium indication from your current insurance company ninety days before your current insurance expires. You'll get push-back on this. Many insurers don't want to play this way. Frankly, getting you the renewal quotes a week before expiration is to your insurer's advantage.

Tell your insurer that you want to settle the issue of the renewal early so that you can make proactive decisions on your insurance. Agree that if the renewal terms are fair, you will not bid your coverage to other insurance companies. You cannot, however, wait until the last minute to get information.

At the same time, discuss other insurers with your agent. Have a plan in place so that if your current insurer does not perform (either their renewal offer is unacceptable or they are unwilling to provide an early indication of premium) you are ready to work with your agent to find other insurers to protect you.

★ Negotiate Your Renewal, Whatever Path You Take

There are several common parts to whatever path you take in the chart above. The most important thing is to always negotiate with insurers before you bind coverage. Premium setting is an art, not a science. Insurers have guidelines for pricing and coverage offerings. There is always room for negotiation.

Underwriters can debit your premiums by 25 percent in most cases. They can also credit your premiums by 25 percent. Right there is a 50 percent swing in premium that is at the discretion of the underwriter. Every insurance company has multiple subsidiary insurers. Those subsidiary companies have different rating structures and plans. Think of Subsidiary Insurer A as being the preferred insurer (with lower rates), and Subsidiary Insurer B as being the standard rated insurer.

Between standard and preferred, debits and credits, insurers have the ability to charge one bank $50K (average rates), an identical bank $31,875 (preferred rates), and a third bank $71,875 (sub-standard rates)—all for the same coverage.

Said another way, the same insurer can choose to charge you $31,875, $50K, or $71,875 for your insurance. Underwriter's choice, insurer preference, your desirability, and (perhaps most importantly) what the insurer thinks it needs to do to keep or get your business.

Premium Options For Your Insurer – How Much Can They Charge?

Insurers have wide latitude in the premiums they charge.

Standard Rates
Base Manual Rates: $50K
Insurer Rating Program Factor: 1.00
Schedule Credits: 1.00
Final Premium: $50K

Sub-Standard Rates
Base Manual Rates: $50K
Insurer Rating Program Factor: 1.15
Schedule Credits: 1.25
Final Premium: $71,875

Preferred Rates
Base Manual Rates: $50K
Insurer Rating Program Factor: 0.85
Schedule Credits: 0.75
Final Premium: $31,875

Negotiate your premiums. Negotiate the coverage. Ask for coverage enhancements while keeping the premium the same.

Negotiation before coverage is bound is the most underused tool in insurance buying.

Path Two: You Can Consider Other Agents, But Do You Want/ Need To?

Your insurance agent should be an important part of your risk management team. Here is the real test:

Imagine you're standing in front of the smoldering hulk that was once your main office. The fire was fast and devastating. Is your insurance agent the person you want standing next to you?

If your answer is anything but an immediate and resounding "Yes!" then it's time to think about finding a new insurance agent (or a great bank insurance consultant).

Have You Bid Your Insurance Recently?

Competition among agents and insurers is the key to getting the best price, coverage, and service. Nothing pushes us to perform better than the nudge of competitive pressures.

Competition means that nobody is sure who will win, and everyone could lose.

Having your insurance agent get multiple quotes from many insurers injects some competition into the process. However, having two agents fighting it out means that the gloves are off, and everyone is in there scrapping for your business.

One agent with multiple insurers is not pushed to get everything from the insurers; the agent may get what he or she can but is not pushed to get everything.

One agent quoting multiple insurers can get away with accepting the quotes he or she is given and presenting them to you.

When there are multiple insurance agents competing for your business, multiple phone calls are made. Supervisors are called in. Everyone scrambles because they have no idea what the other agent is presenting, and nobody wants to lose.

When multiple agents are involved in your account, vying for your business, insurers are called at the last minute and asked for a bit more credit and a bit more coverage.

However, you are not well served by bidding your insurance every year. The process is exhausting for agents, and it involves the resources of your bank. Agents that compete and do not win will resent the work they put in to no reward. The insurance company underwriters will also feel left out. Bidding every three to five years is an effective course. It gives you a chance to see the work your agent does for you. You get to build a relationship with an agent and insurer.

Renewing When You Don't Bid

So you're in between bids, meaning that you bid your coverage within the last few years. Follow the process I described above in the discussion of what to do when you can't change agents:

- Start the renewal process early.

- Insist on getting premium and coverage indications from your agent and insurer ninety days before your program expiration date.

- Talk with your agent about other insurers.

- Negotiate, negotiate, negotiate.

Agent Selection Process

The agent selection process is an important part of changing agents or going to bid. In either case, you want to choose from a pool of the best agents.

If you are changing agents, your goal is a pool of agents from which you will pick one to bring you proposals from the insurers he or she thinks are best for your risk exposures and appetites.

If you are bidding your insurance, your goal is a pool of agents from which you will select a few who will bring you proposals from selected insurers.

Turn the page for details on the agent selection process.

Chapter Twenty-Four: Agent Selection Process

Agent Selection Process, Step One: Building Your List of Agents

The agent selection process starts with you building a list of possible participants. In most cases, you will include your current agent. You may have agents who approached you about quoting on your business. You may know of agents who specialize in bank insurance in your region. You may have customers or other business associates who are in the insurance business.

Sources of Agents for the Selection Process

– Your current agent
– Agents you have worked with in the past
– Customers who are agents
– Check with your state banking association
– Talk with friendly competitor banks
– Agents in your community
– Referral from board members

You should have at least three agents on your list. Five is a better number. I have never had more than ten—though it wouldn't be wrong if you really have that many agents you want to consider.

There is no downside to including an agent at this point. In fact, many banks like to have a large list at the start so that they can be looked at in their community as considering a wide range of options, including all the local talent.

Agent Selection Process, Step Two: Send Questionnaire to Agents

Contact each agent on your list by email. Attach the questionnaire shown below (customized for your bank). The purpose of the questionnaire is to learn more about the agents and agencies so that you can move toward your final selections.

(Go to www.ScottSimmonds.com/bankbook2 to get this form in digital format so you don't have to type it up.)

Prepare the form by giving the agents an idea of who you are and what you do. Give the agents information about your bank. You need to share some data here—asset size, number of employees, etc.

There is one issue that comes up all the time: should you divulge current premiums or not?

I include the current premiums in the info I send to potential agents, as it puts everyone on an even field with knowledge of the current situation. Your current agent and insurer know where they are now—they have no idea where the competitors will come in. Giving the competitors premium info does not jeopardize your current insurer. Your objective is best coverage, best price, and best service. A competitive bid process gets that for you. Nobody knows the bids, so they have to come up with their best price.

Knowing your current premium does not really help the competing agents. However, it makes them feel like you are being open with them.

**BANK INSURANCE PROPOSAL / AGENT SELECTION
PRE-QUALIFICATION QUESTIONNAIRE**

Note: You may submit this information in any format you wish as long as the information provided is complete. You do not need to use this form.

General Information About Your Firm

Your Firm's Name:

Mailing Address:

Physical Location:

Telephone   Fax:

Name of Contact Person: Email:

How many bank clients does your organization currently serve?

What is your approximate premium volume of bank business?

Account Management Team

Please attach a brief résumé for each person who would be handling our account. As a minimum, please be sure the following information is included:

Name and position	Length of time in insurance business
Licenses held	Length of time in your employment
Insurance work experience	Insurance designations earned
Specific experience with banks	Specific skills or expertise
Expected role on this account	

Please describe any specialized services which your firm has to offer, and which you feel would enhance your position in our evaluation.

References

List at least three bank clients or clients who have similar exposures.

Name:

      Contact Name:

      Phone:

Name:

      Contact Name:

      Phone:

Name:

      Contact Name:

      Phone:

Any reference you provide may be contacted without notice to you.

Agents and insurers feel that they are shooting in the dark without the current premium numbers. It really tells them nothing, but it makes them feel more comfortable.

Many bankers feel that showing the current premium hurts the integrity of the bid process. I find that the reality is that it makes insurers work harder. Strange but true, in my experience. My advice is to give the current premium.

Send the agent your customized form as a word processing document attached to an email. This will make it easier for the agent to respond.

I insist on email responses to my questionnaires. You can be more relaxed by allowing email, fax, and mail replies.

Some agents will want to meet with you prior to completing the form. Put them off.

The form is designed to give you a true feel for the agency. Can they follow instructions? Do they meet deadlines? Also, the form doesn't require much effort on the agent's part. Some brokers have a form they have used for other such projects. As long as I get the information I want about the agency, I don't get too clutched about what format the agents use to respond—so long as they reply by email.

Give the agents a relatively short deadline-between five and ten days. Nobody needs more than that. This is not a tough process.

I suggest a date and time deadline—I usually say noon on a specific day.

Agent Selection Process, Step Three: Review the Responses

With responses in hand, you need to figure out your next step. Recall that you now have two options:

1. Select a single agent, allowing him or her access to all insurers.

2. Select several agents, moving to a bid process.

Your choice for option one might be your current agent, or you might select a new agent.

Here are the questions I use in the review of the questionnaires. No single question tells me the right agents to take on. I look at the overall quality. Some clients have assigned point values to each of the following criteria. Is there any doubt that some bank CEOs/CFOs have accounting backgrounds?

Did the agent acknowledge my initial email? I want to know if the agent follows good business practices. Acknowledging emails and expressing some level of enthusiasm at being asked to participate tells me what type of business person I am dealing with.

Did the agent reply on time? I'm pretty tough on this one. If your reply is late and you don't tell me why, how can I trust you to respond to a claim?

What is the agent's experience in the banking industry? The world of banking insurance is unique. An agent who has bank insurance experience is valuable.

Who did the agent use for references? Are the references current clients? Are they banks? Are they known to you?

What are the lead agent's credentials? Who is the prime manager of your account? What is his experience? What insurance educational programs has he been involved in? Does he have an advanced insurance industry professional designation? (I am partial to the Chartered Property Casualty Underwriter designation, CPCU. It is a rigorous program that takes several years to complete. There are certainly great insurance people without a CPCU designation. However, I have met few CPCUs that are not dedicated to the insurance industry.)

Does the agent have a team of people who will work with him or her? How many? Where are they located? How easy will they be to contact? What are the team members' duties?

What are the credentials of the team? Who is working on the team? What experience do they have? There should be competent backup to the prime agent (a.k.a. a producer—a horrible term, I think). Many agents are out of the office frequently. Who is there day-to-day to answer your billing questions and move paper for you?

How many employees does the agency have? A two person insurance agency provides a different level of service from a twenty-person office. The size of an organization is important, as it tells us something about market strength. A small insurance agency may not have the heft to get the difficult coverage issues of claims settled with an insurance company.

Is the agent a local independent business or a part of a regional/national agency? There are advantages and disadvantages to dealing with bigger agencies—as with every type of firm.

What insurers did the agent request access to and why? Take a piece of paper and build a chart. Each agent will be a column. List the insurers each agent has asked to use under that agent's column. Some agents will list a single insurer. Some will list ten.

There are three different types of insurers listed on the questionnaire—bank specialty (i.e., bond, directors' & officers', e-banking), standard (i.e., property, liability, auto, umbrella), and workers' compensation. Some insurers will offer all three categories. Some may only offer one.

Make three sections on your chart, one for each type of insurance.

Review the agents' selections. Are there common insurers? Did one insurer only show up on one agent's list?

With the above info, you have a growing picture of each agent.

Agent Selection Process, Step Four: Gather More Info

You may have enough info now to make your decision. Probably not.

In most cases, there will be questions you'd like to ask. Perhaps you need clarification. Pick up the phone.

A phone interview is often quite telling. If you leave a message, how long does it take the agent to call you back? How does the agent respond to questions? Is he long-winded or does he get to the point?

Here are some good phone interview questions for agents:

– You selected ABC Mutual as your first choice of insurer. Tell me why. What is your experience with that insurer?

– Main Street Bank is on your reference list. Tell me about your work for them. (How much does the agent tell you? Does she divulge confidential information?)

– If I have a claim, will I work with you or your claim department?

– I assume you are out of the office a fair amount. When I'm a client, do I call you or a customer service person with my questions?

Agent Selection Process, Step Five: Interviews

The first question for step five is: are you done now? Is there one agent who stands above the others?

Perhaps you now realize the actual quality of your current agent. Maybe you see just how terrible he really is. It's possible that you now know that you want to move to another agent.

It would not surprise me if you are not ready yet. It does happen, though not often. Sometimes the insurance buyer looks at the field before him and decides to just stay with the current agent. If that's you, notify the other agents and get your agent moving forward for you.

If you have decided on a new agent and want to fire your current agent, do it now. Get the new agent working for you and notify the agents you did not select.

Firing Your Insurance Agent

Firing your insurance agent is like firing an employee. It should rarely be a surprise for either party. Prior to the termination, there should have been conversations over poor performance. Sometimes, however, insurance buyers are just not aware of how bad their agents really are (or they have been deluding themselves).

Once the decision is made to end an insurance relationship, pull the trigger quickly. Hire slow, fire fast. If in the middle of the agent selection process you become convinced that you will not select your current agent, do not tease the agent along. It causes him to do more work with no hope of success. Further, it limits what other agents can do for you, thus harming your chance for greatest value.

If you have any doubts, I urge you to continue on with the selection process.

At this point, there are probably some agents who are standing out. Maybe you have identified agents you know you cannot work with. If you cannot pick one single agent for yourself yet, you can undoubtedly narrow the field a bit. Cull the pack to two or three.

Perhaps these are the two or three agents you want in the bid process. Consider in-person interviews as a way to narrow the field further.

Call the successful agents to set up a presentation meeting. Be sure to call those agents who completed a questionnaire but were not selected. They put effort into the first phase of this project and deserve the courtesy of a call.

Your interviews should all be held on the same day. Tell each agent that he or she has thirty minutes. Schedule the presentations forty-five minutes apart. This gives you some time to discuss each presentation with other members of your team and builds in time for presentations running a bit longer. Don't put off calling the agents who were not invited to make presentations. Procrastination here will only make the calls tougher.

Preinterview Meetings

Some agents will want to meet with you before they make their presentations. They'll want to get to know you and your business. Frankly, it's the good agents who will ask for such a meeting. I don't ask the agents for a meeting. I let them come up with the idea. Remember, you're trying to get into the agents' heads to see how interested they are in your business. What they don't do may be as important as what they do.

Plan to spend about sixty minutes with an agent in a pre-presentation meeting. Don't let the agent talk a great deal about himself or his agency. The purpose of the meeting is for the agent to get to know you so he can do a great job in his presentation.

The Interviews

In most cases, you'll want to include several of your key people in the sessions. Depending on the size and structure of your bank, your corporate officers and human resource managers may be involved.

Some call these agent presentations "dog and pony shows." It's the agent's opportunity to show off his or her qualifications and expertise. Different agents take different approaches to the presentation. Some will bore you with an overview of the history of their agency or give a live version of their résumé. Good agents will focus on the value they will provide you as your insurance agent. The best will provide you with a case study as an example of how they serve clients.

The presentation meeting is the agency's opportunity to tell its story. From that meeting, you will select the right agency.

At the conclusion of the presentation, have questions prepared to ask all the prospective agents. Here are some examples:

– Describe a situation where you provided exceptional client service.

– We are also interviewing the ABC Agency and folks from DEF Insurance. Why should we pick you?

– Tell me about a recent situation where you lost a client.

– Describe your service team and how a request for a certificate of insurance will be handled.

– What is your process for handling a small claim?

Some questions need to be asked of each agency. You will want to compare answers by each participant:

– Will you provide us with an annual account review? When in the year will this take place?

– How will you ensure that we have renewal quotes at least twenty–one days before our renewal?

– What claims management services will you provide?

– What loss control services will you provide?

You're trying to get the agent talking about his or her services and approach to the business. You want to talk with the person who will be working on your account. In many cases, a supervisor or principal of the agency will attend the meeting. Don't let the boss hog the spotlight. You want to hear from the people who will be working on your account on a day-to-day basis: the service reps.

I try to get the team off their scripts so I can have a conversation. Ask probing questions that cause the presenters to think and speak outside of their comfort zones. These people will have millions of dollars of your assets in their care. You want sharp people on your team.

After the Presentation

On occasion, your choice will be easy. One agency may be the clear winner. Don't jump too fast. Pick your top two agents and ask each for a one-page, written service plan for the first year he or she will be handling your account. Explain that the choice is very difficult and that you need a bit more information.

Depending on geography, consider meeting the agents at their offices. It gives you a chance to learn more about the agency and its culture. Get to know the agent. Talk more with the service team. Perhaps go to lunch with people from the agency.

Agent Selection Process, Step Six: The Decision

After the questionnaire, the presentation, and the written service plan, you should have a good idea of who you'd like to work with.

If you're having trouble with the decision, here are a few questions to ask yourself:

- Which agency would I like in my corner if I were in a claim dispute with my insurance company?

- Which agent seems to be the most comfortable with the banking industry and the unique exposures presented?

- If my attorney has a question about my insurance coverage, which agent do I feel confident about providing accurate information and assistance?

- If my administrative center were destroyed by a fire, which agent would I want on my team?

Here again you should be asking yourself if you want to pick *the* agent for you or if you want a bid process.

Picking *The* Agent

If the agent selection process has you at a place where you have decided to move forward with a single agent (perhaps your current agent), then contact that agent and set the expectations for the management of the renewal. Get a commitment on when proposals will be delivered to you, what insurers will be contacted, and how you expect the relationship to progress.

Notify the unsuccessful agents, and move forward with the renewal.

If you want to move forward with multiple agents in a bid process, see the next chapter.

My Approach

I have seen the process above be successful for bankers who are managing their own renewal. As a bank insurance consultant, I take a slightly different approach from what I prescribe above. After thirty years, I know many of the agents with whom I work. I know what to look for. I know that special brand of BS known as "Insurance BS."

I use the same questionnaire I have given you. I also gauge the needs of my bank client and their willingness to really go through a bid process. I push and goad my clients to be sure they are serious about changing agents. Often, what started out as a bid process ends up with me pushing the bank to admit that they will not leave their current agent—thus saving everyone involved a great deal of time, effort, and angst.

I throw agents out of the selection process for minor infractions. I will not recommend an agent who does not show me a firm interest in my client's business. I will not recommend an agent who is not 100 percent dedicated to insurance as a profession. If the agent mentions retirement in any of our conversations, he is out.

I question an agent's dedication to the insurance business if he or she has been in the business for more than five years and has not at least started on an industry designation like CPCU (Chartered Property and Casualty Underwriter). Agents in the business for more than ten years without a CPCU are, in my mind, suspect.

Frankly, I have gotten pretty good at spending fifteen minutes on the phone with an agent and predicting his or her success with my clients.

I rarely allow preinterview meetings where the agent gets to learn about the bank. If I think my client will benefit from getting to know the agent, I do not attend the sessions.

I am acutely aware of the importance of an insurance buyer being comfortable with a particular agent. I often set up situations for the agent and banker to interact. That usually comes in the bid process, though.

If we do decide to have agent interviews, I keep them to twenty minutes. I am ruthless about keeping agents to the allotted time. I warn the agents ahead of time that they will not be allowed to go over. I suggest that they not bring any props or presentation items. I suggest that the boss stays home. I want the agent and the service team. I want the bank to meet with the day-to-day people who will help them manage risk.

I have questions prepared for the session, and coach the bankers in the room on how this session should work. I take full responsibility for being the bad guy.

In my process, as a consultant, interviews are for getting people off the list. If, after the interview, we still cannot agree on who to work with, I suggest that the insurance buyer meets with the agent at the agent's office. I do not attend those meetings.

As they say on the TV action shows, I'm a professional. Do not try this at home.

Chapter Twenty-Five: Multiple Agents Bidding Multiple Insurers

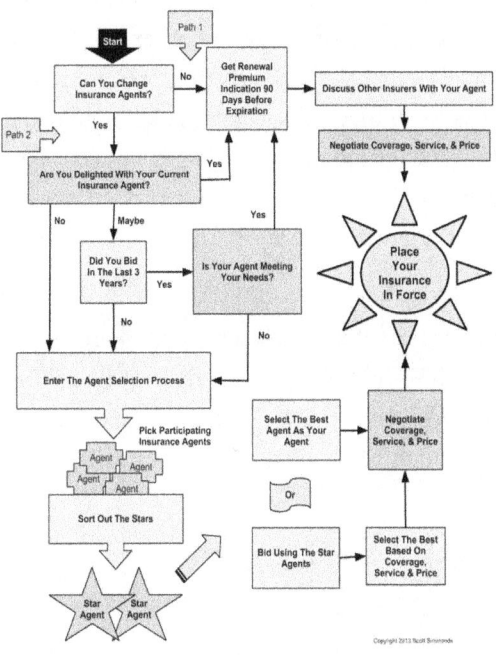

If you have been following along in previous chapters, you have moved down the left side of the diagram, picked a bunch of agents, sorted them out, come up with the stars, and decided (from the last chapter) that you did not want to pick a single agent.

You're at the bottom of the diagram above: "Bid Using the Star Agents."

In this process, you will end up getting proposals from the star agents, picking the best, and allowing that agent to place insurance in force with the insurer he or she proposed.

Here's a detailed picture of the bid process from the broker selection process described in the last chapter.

Bid Process, Step One: Insurer Assignment

Now that you have your agents selected, you must assign insurance companies to each agent.

In property and casualty insurance, insurers limit agent access. If Agent A contacts Podunk Insurance Company, no other insurance agent will be able to get a quote from Podunk. Many call this process market blocking—only one agent has access to an insurer. Other agents are blocked unless they move the "authority" to another agent by getting a broker of record letter signed by the insurance buyer. The broker of record letter moves the authority and access from the first agent to the agent in possession of the letter. The first agent loses access.

Confused? It's understandable! It's a confusing process. I think the whole thing is anticompetitive and wrong. I've been fighting it for twenty-five years. It is a tradition that protects sloppy agents at the expense of quality. However, it is the system we have to work with in most states.

Market Blocking Is Anticompetitive

For more than twenty-five years, I have been fighting the idea that an insurer will only provide a quote to a single agent for a business. Here is a letter I wrote several years ago, published by The Standard, an insurance industry publication:

To the Editor,

The insurance business needs to lose a vestige of the insurance marketplace of the last century. Let's become friendlier to competition and the free market.

For my thirty years in the insurance business, I have seen insurance companies engage in a market practice that is anticompetitive, restrictive to the free insurance market, and just plain wrong.

From the insurance buyer's perspective, the practice is called "market blocking." It is the tradition that an insurer will only provide a proposal to a single agent—blocking all other agents from accessing that market for that insurance buyer.

For as long as anyone I know can remember, property and casualty insurance companies have only provided proposals of insurance to a single agent for a particular insurance buyer.

If Brown Company wants a quote from Insurance Agent A and Insurance Agent B, Peerless Insurance will only provide a quote to the first agent with applications. The same is true of Hanover, Acadia, MEMIC, OneBeacon, Hartford, Travelers, Chubb, AIG, Philadelphia Insurance, Maine Mutual, and every other insurer I can think of.

Agent A and Agent B will not be able to deliver a business insurance proposal from the same insurer. For many agents and insurance buyers, this means that there is little real choice, as different insurers have different appetites. Most agents have been in the situation where they are unable to quote an account because other agents have reserved the insurers who have an interest in the account.

In some cases, agents game the system by firing off applications to insurers for no other reason than to keep other agents from participating in a bid.

This practice of blocking limits competition and therefore has a negative impact on the marketplace. Restricting the ability of agents to compete for business leads to higher prices for insurance buyers.

This is clearly anticompetitive and allows certain insurance agents and brokers to control the marketplace without value to the insurance buyer. It is certainly true that the insurance buyer can assign the insurer to another agent. Two agents can't quote the same insurer though.

Imagine the price of any product without competition. Let's open up the marketplace.

I am not advocating regulation. I abhor government intervention in the marketplace, and am a consistent and vocal opponent of rules and laws imposed on any industry. In my experience, regulation is usually couched in terms of protecting consumers when in reality the protection provided is for the industry itself or for protecting regulator jobs. Regulations almost always restrict competition in some way, and that is against the interests of consumers. Further, government intervention always limits freedoms.

I am asking that insurance companies end the anachronistic practice of market blocking and allow multiple agents to present quotes for a single insurance buyer. Allow the insurance buyer to see the quality and professionalism of the agent through open competition.

Not only is open competition good for the insurance buyer, but it is also healthy for the high quality agent. Fewer restrictions on competition means that more buyers will see the professionalism of the agents they work with.

Insurance companies also benefit. More competition means more good business will come to insurers who will have a better chance of winning exceptional accounts.

Further, I call for an end to state anti-rebating laws. Allow individual insurance producers to determine the terms of the sale of a policy. If the agent wants to provide a lower premium to an insured by cutting commissions, why not? Does a restaurant set a meal price? Can a lawyer not set her own fees? Let an insurance agent do the same!

I'm sure that many can come up with reasons to retain these market restrictive practices. None of them, I dare say, have anything to do with what is in the best interest of the insurance buyer.

Allow insurance buyers to judge the quality of the agent and the coverage offered. Allow agents to compete freely. Remove restrictions on competition between agents. Allow quality and not protectionism to rule the insurance market.

From the "Agent Selection Questionnaire" you received in the process of selecting participating agents (see sample form in Appendix Two), each agent requested access to specific insurers for bank specialty insurance, standard property and casualty lines, and workers' compensation.

Use that information to complete a matrix of requests—one for each of the three lines of coverage (bank specialty, standard property and casualty, and workers' compensation).

	Current Agent	Agent A	Agent B
First choice			
Second choice			
Third choice			
Fourth choice			

Your current agent will probably ask for the current insurance company. That is almost always granted and becomes his or her first choice.

Are there overlaps with the other agents and your current agent? This may be your chance to further narrow down your choice of agents.

Whenever possible, I recommend that you bid with only two agents—your current agent and the strongest competitor. Having three agents may force you to split up the markets too thinly.

By the way, the market selection process is the single toughest part of the bid process. Assign markets improperly and you may end up hurting the outcome of the bids. At times, you may have to discuss the issues with the participating agents. If one insurance company is the top choice of each agent, consider calling the agents separately and having them make the case for that insurer to supplement their comments in the Agent Selection Questionnaire.

Frankly, in a three-agent bid situation, someone always ends up being ticked off at the assignments. It is possible that one agent will pull out at this point if that person feels incapable of getting a fair shot at the business with the markets assigned to him or her. I never hold such a move against an agent, whose time is valuable, too.

Step Two: Provide Agents With Underwriting Information

You're going to have to put together information on your current insurance program along with claims information and underwriting information. Ask your current agent to help with this process. Most will help you. It may be a touchy subject. Some agents don't want to help the competition. Take the stance that this is part of an agent's job. Failure to cooperate here will be viewed negatively at decision time.

It is possible for each participating agent to build his or her own information. This will mean a great deal more time for you. Push your agent to cooperate.

Underwriting information should include:

- A schedule of all vehicles, mobile equipment, buildings, and other property to be insured. No value is necessary for vehicles. Mobile equipment should show market values (actual cash value). Buildings and personal property should show replacement cost values.

- Five years of insurer loss runs (your current agent can provide these to you).

- Workers' compensation experience modification worksheets for the upcoming year and the current policy period.

- General liability premium basis (e.g., payroll, sales, square footage) based upon the current policy (available from your agent), updated for what is expected in the policy period being quoted.

- Your bank's marketing materials, Web site address, sample brochures, and the like.

- A copy of your employee handbook.

- Applications from your current insurer for directors' and officers', bond, and e-banking insurance coverage. (Most insurers quoting coverage will work from your current insurance company's applications.)

- Other information that may help underwriters to see the bank in a positive light. Some banks provide pictures or video of virtual tours.

Get the underwriting information out to the agents at least one hundred days before the renewal date.

Be clear about when the bids are due to you and what format in which you want the bids presented. If your bank's board of directors is to be involved, add time to your schedule for their input. Specify that bids are due at noon on a specific date at a specific place. Events sometimes transpire to make it difficult for an agent to get bids in on time. You will have to decide if you will allow late bid presentations.

Should You Tell Everyone Your Current Premiums?

Obviously there are two schools of thought—tell and don't tell. Those in favor of "don't tell" say it keeps everyone on their toes. Everyone, that is, except your current agent. It's an advantage to your current agent to have the competing agents in the dark over your premiums. It's not a fair advantage.

I say, "tell." In my bid specifications, I include information on the current premiums by line of coverage. To me, this puts everyone on the same level. Everyone knows the current premiums. Nobody knows the proposed premiums.

Other Rules of the Game

Another question you will have to deal with in a bid is: will your current agent get the last shot at your business? It is a common practice for insurance buyers to give their current agents a last chance to match their competitors' prices.

The logic goes like this: "We have done business together for a long time. My agent has done a great job and deserves every opportunity to keep our business."

If this is how you look at your agent, then why are you bidding your insurance? Don't put the other agents through the exercise of bidding if your current agent is going to get a last chance to hit the target.

The bid process should be fair and upfront. If, at the end of the process, you plan to give your current agent the advantage of a second chance, then you should reconsider going through the bid procedure.

Be clear and upfront about how the bid is going to be handled. If your current agent gets a second chance, you should tell the other agents at the beginning of the process. Give them a chance to walk away before they invest twenty to fifty hours on your bid process.

To me, the only fair bid is a bid that is decided based on the proposals presented. Notice I didn't say that the best price wins. You should make your decision on services, coverage, and price.

Sample Bid Rules

Here is a statement you can provide to the agents participating in your insurance bid process:

We promise to deal openly and fairly with all agents and insurance companies.

Problems rarely "take care of themselves." If you have a concern, issue, or problem, bring it up sooner rather than later.

Your proposals are confidential. We believe that an insurance marketplace that is fair and upfront is in everybody's best interest. We will never reveal or share any competitive information you provide with any other agent or company prior to receiving their proposal.

In our bidding process, we allow the competing agents to review "current" policies and pricing. We believe that this puts everyone on an even playing field. Everyone knows the current year's price. Nobody knows the bidding price when they submit proposals.

We do not give "second chances" in bids or proposals. We expect your best work from the start. Discrepancies will be addressed without revealing any other participant's position.

We set deadlines in an effort to make the process work better for us. If you are going to miss a deadline, we are better off knowing as soon as possible.

Any proposal you provide will be reviewed on the basis of coverage, price, and services offered. We are under no obligation to purchase insurance based on price alone.

The information we provide to you is accurate to the best of our knowledge.

Information Meetings

Encourage participating agents to meet with you to gather information needed for the bid. It is also your chance to get to know the agents. Good agents will request these meetings. They will want to spend some time with you and the other decision makers.

This is the agent's chance to learn about you. You also have the opportunity to see how the agent thinks and how or she he approaches the business. Competing agents may request different information or additional documents. Do your best to comply. I would urge you not to tell other agents (or your current agent) what information competitors requested. Exposure identification is an important part of what an agent is expected to do. Tipping the hand of one agent hurts the competitive process.

Don't play favorites with the agents. If you're going to do that, why bother involving the others?

Bid Presentation

In the beginning of the bid process, you gave each agent a deadline. Allow agents to present their bids in any format they wish. Some will email, some will mail, and some will present in person.

Here's another opportunity to learn about how the agent approaches the business.

Comparing Bids

Now comes the hard part. You have to compare the different proposals. I use two tools. One is objective. The other is subjective.

For coverage comparison, I find a matrix is useful. Make a chart with columns for each bid. Down the left side, list coverage limits and issues. A sample form is included in Appendix Two. You can also use the information in the various proposals for information on issues you should consider.

If you're having trouble with the decision, here are a few subjective questions to ask yourself:

- Which agency would I like in my corner if there were a claim dispute with my insurance company?

- Which agent seems to be the most comfortable with the banking industry and the unique exposures that our bank presents?

- If my attorney had a question about my insurance coverage, which agent am I most confident would provide accurate information and assistance?

- If my administrative center were destroyed by a fire, which agent would I want on my team?

After Bid Interview

In cases where you are still undecided, it may be helpful to interview the agents again. Here are some general tips:

– Don't divulge the other agents' pricing.

– Don't allow the agents to amend their price.

– What coverage is included in one proposal but absent from another? Ask the agents why there is a difference. "Bill, you didn't include coverage for business income. Any reason why? Your competition included the coverage."

– Affirm the service schedule that the agent promised. Will there be annual reviews, or will you meet quarterly?

Bid Ethics

The bid process is filled with opportunities for misunderstanding and abuse. As I've stated before, 85 percent of all insurance bids industry-wide result in the incumbent agent and insurer retaining the business. Many agents are no longer bidding insurance coverage because of the odds against them. Many choose to compete only on a broker/agent selection basis.

Here are some general thoughts about bidding:

– Treat all agents the same. Don't play favorites.

– Promise the competing agents that the current agent will not get a "last shot" at the bid.

– Be upfront with each agent about your process and approach. Nobody can claim foul if the rules are spelled out ahead of time.

Chapter Twenty-Six: Property Claims Help

The most common bank insurance claim is damage to buildings or business property.

Vandals paint graffiti on the side of one of your branch offices.
A customer's vehicle hits the overhang on your drive-up window.
An electrical circuit overheats, causing a fire at your administrative center.
A windstorm damages the roof of your main office.

Should You Turn the Claim In?

In a prior section, I discussed the use of deductibles to reduce your property insurance premiums. A high deductible means that small claims will not be insured. Your insurer will want you to report all incidents that damage your property. I recommend a more conservative approach to my clients: don't report small property claims.

As each renewal approaches, insurers review your claims to determine that year's premium. Many small property claims on your account will cause premiums to rise, as insurers hate claim frequency. Protect your bank by paying small claims without reporting them to the insurance company. (Always report workers' compensation, liability, and auto claims.)

The above being said, once you decide to move forward without your insurer, you will have a very difficult time getting the insurance company involved. If you find later that the damage is more extensive than you originally thought, you could be on your own to pay it. Use caution.

Protect the Property From Further Loss

You are responsible for the protection of your property after a loss. If a windstorm damages your roof, call a contractor for temporary repairs. If a fire has destroyed a part of your building, protect the rest of the building from damage by weather or thieves. Perhaps temporary repairs are in order. Perhaps you need to hire a security firm. Move undamaged property to a safe location for storage. Save receipts for what you spend, and submit them to your insurance company for reimbursement. Do not make permanent repairs without first consulting your agent. Your insurance company may give you a hard time if it is not a part of the rebuilding process.

Contact Your Insurance Agent as Quickly as Possible

Once you decide to involve your insurer, quickly inform him or her of your loss. In smaller claims, the adjuster will contact you by phone. Larger claims will involve regular visits from the adjuster.

Document the Damage

Take pictures of the damage. Save newspaper articles. Damaged property should not be discarded before your insurance company gives you permission.

Document Your Expenses

Most bank insurance programs will include coverage for extra expenses you incur to get back into operation quickly. Advertisements of temporary locations, refitting another location to accommodate displaced employees, and increased cost of operations are all a part of your extra expense loss.

Document All Activity

Every conversation with the insurance company adjuster should be documented and confirmed. If you're asked to get estimates and told you can remove the rubble, send an email to the adjuster (with a copy to your agent) confirming that you will be contacting contractors and will have the rubble removed.

Act as if you are the project manager and the adjuster is a key part of the team. Work together. If things move in a direction you are not comfortable with, immediately involve your agent.

★ Expect Complexity and a Bumpy Road

Only the smallest property claims are simple. Work through the process expecting some misunderstandings and miscommunication. Head off problems down the road by documenting, confirming, and being active in the adjustment of your claim. Property claims are construction projects with more emotion and urgency.

All Claims Adjustments are Negotiations

The insurance policy outlines the coverage provided. Rarely are property claims handled 100 percent as the policy intended. You may want to add a third floor to the building that will replace the damaged structure. Perhaps you will not occupy the building as a branch but will use it as an administrative office. Perhaps you will not rebuild the building at all.

Work with the adjuster through the negotiations of your insurance claim. Bring your agent into the picture. Perhaps other advisers such as consultants, contractors, and lawyers can provide helpful input.

Involve Your Agent in the Process

While most agents don't deal directly with claims, most will step in when a problem exists. Helping you with the process is a part of their job. Use their resources.

Chapter Twenty-Seven: Liability Claims Help

Report all accidents involving injuries or damage to property owned by others to your insurance company as soon as possible.

Train your branch staff to respond to slip and fall accidents and to report the incidents to your insurer. If you want a central reporting structure, make sure claims reported to the insurers are not delayed in the process.

In the banking world, the most common general liability claim is a slip and fall accident. Most general liability claims occur in parking lots, lobbies, and drive-through teller areas.

Document the Accident

As soon as you (or your people) are aware of an accident where a customer or member of the public is hurt, the report should be sent to the insurance company. Take pictures of the location of the accident as soon as possible. (All your locations should have a camera. Disposable cameras work well for documentation purposes.) Document the conditions that existed. Get the contact info of all injured people and witnesses.

Correct any hazards that caused the accident.

Follow Up With Adjusters

Liability claims can take months to resolve. Contact the insurance company adjuster every few months to learn the status.

Chapter Twenty-Eight: Automobile Claims Help

Report all auto accidents involving injuries or damage to property owned by others to your insurance company as soon as possible—from the accident scene, if it's practical. Fast reporting is vital when there are serious injuries. In some cases, your insurer will dispatch a rapid response adjuster to the scene.

Train your employees on the importance of rapid reporting. If you want a central reporting structure, make sure claims reported to the insurers are not delayed in the process.

Auto accidents are the area of greatest liability exposure for large losses in the banking world.

Any employee driving on bank business (i.e., to conferences, educational seminars, chamber of commerce events, sales calls, etc.) can lead to bank liability for an accident.

Document the Accident

Take pictures of the location of the accident as soon as possible. (All bank vehicles should have a camera in an emergency kit, along with the phone numbers of your insurance agent and your insurance company's twenty-four-hour hotline. Disposable cameras work well for documentation purposes.) Document the conditions that existed. Get the contact info of all injured people and witnesses.

Employees who regularly drive their own vehicles on bank business should be trained to report accidents quickly. They, too, should be supplied with a disposable camera and insurance company contact info. They are covered by their own insurance for damage to their vehicle and their liability. The bank's liability is covered by the bank's insurance.

Follow Up With Adjusters

Stay in touch with your insurance company adjuster on the status of all claims. Your involvement may make the difference between a claim that drags on and one with a fast resolution.

Chapter Twenty-Nine: Workers' Compensation Claims Help

The workers' compensation claims process is largely determined by state law. Your insurance company will have forms and procedures to follow to report new incidents. Most have phone or Internet reporting systems.

Frankly, the biggest problem I have with my bank clients and workers' compensation is that you don't have enough claims to get used to the claims process.

Report Claims Quickly

Develop a claims reporting system in each of your locations. Employees should know to whom they should report incidents. Managers should know where reports should be filed. Fast claim reporting to your insurer means an overall better outcome.

Have a Designated Physician/Medical Facility for Employee Injuries

Many states allow employers to designate a specific physician or medical center for the first few weeks of an employee's injury. This increased control allows specialists in workplace injuries to provide effective treatment for injuries such as soft tissue injuries (strained back) and repetitive motion claims (carpal tunnel and tendinitis issues).

Remote branches may need a separate designated medical facility.

Reporting claims promptly will improve your insurer's ability to manage claims. You end up saving premium dollars, and your employees get better care.

Follow Up With Your Adjuster

If you average four or five workers' compensation claims a year, have one adjuster for all of your claims. Tell your insurer that you want to build a relationship with the adjuster handling your account. You want the adjuster to have a working knowledge of your approach to business and workers' compensation injuries. You want the adjuster to be a part of your team.

Review all open claims once a quarter with your agent and adjuster. The conversation is simple. Find out what has been done and what is going to be done. Follow up on any action plans. You want your claims to be handled as a priority by your insurance company.

Have a Return to Work Program

Work aggressively to bring employees back to work. Have a light-duty program available. Work with your employees' doctors and adjuster to find meaningful work your injured employees can do.

Chapter Thirty: D&O and Employment Practices Claims Help

We all know when we have had an auto accident. A fire is a clear indication of a property claim. But when do you report a claim under your directors' and officers' or employment practices insurance policies?

What is a Claim?

Here are the definitions of a claim under one insurer's contract:

"Claim" means a director and officer claim, an entity claim, an employment practices claim, a lenders' liability claim, a securities claim, and a trust department claim.

"Director and officer claim" means a demand or proceeding against a director or officer for a wrongful act other than an employment practices claim, a lenders' liability claim, a securities claim, or a trust-department claim.

"Employment practices claim" means a demand or proceeding against either a director or officer, or the company (if so indicated on the declarations) for a wrongful act in connection with any actual or alleged:

– wrongful refusal to employ a qualified applicant for employment;

– wrongful failure to promote a qualified employee;

– wrongful demotion, negligent evaluation, negligent reassignment, or wrongful discipline of any employee;

– wrongful termination of employment, including retaliatory or constructive discharge;

– harassment, coercion, discrimination or humiliation of an employee or applicant for employment as a consequence of race, color, creed, national origin, marital status, medical condition, gender, age, physical appearance, physical and/or mental impairment, pregnancy, sexual orientation, or sexual preference; or

– oral or written publication of material that slanders, defames, or libels an employee or violates or invades an employee's right of privacy.

"Entity claim" means a demand or proceeding against the company (if so indicated on the declarations) for a wrongful act other than an employment practices claim, a lenders' liability claim, a securities claim, or a trust department claim.

The D&O policy deals with claims against the directors, officers, and entity (the bank) for "wrongful acts."

Here is the same insurer's definition of wrongful act:

"Any actual or alleged act, error, neglect, omission, misstatement, misleading statement, or breach of duty which shall have been committed or attempted, or which shall be alleged to have been committed or attempted. ..."

The policy goes on to say that claims must be reported to the insurer as soon as "practicable."

When Should a Claim Be Reported?

The easiest way to look at claim reporting is the following:

Have you been sent or given a notice of a hearing, trial, or administrative proceeding for an act that may be covered by your insurance?

Have you received a notice demanding compensation for a wrongful act?

If the answer is yes to either of the above, report the claim. This means that an attorney's letter stating that his client was fired unlawfully is a claim and must be reported to the insurer. A notice from your state's Equal Opportunity Board is a claim. Formal notice of a lawsuit is also a claim.

Review the definition of "claim" in your policy. Does the allegation have to be in writing?

Some insurers' definitions of "claim" require that the notice be in writing. The above policy does not. A customer who walks into your office and demands $10K, alleging that a loan was improperly refused, is (under the definition above) a claim.

Failure to report a claim in a timely fashion can result in the insurance company denying coverage. In most cases, there is little reason to delay the reporting of a claim.

Notice that the above doesn't address the issue of claims under your deductible amount. Most banks have deductibles well over $50K. Many of the allegations made against financial institutions are under the amount where insurance steps in. If there is even the slightest chance that the claim (payment to the claimant and defense costs) may exceed the deductible, my advice is to report the claim.

Some insurers want all "claims" reported. Others only want to hear if you exceed the deductible. Work with your insurer to establish an understanding of what should be reported.

How Do You Report a Claim?

Most insurance policies will have a specific section dedicated to claim reporting. There will be a specific address, phone number, and fax number where you send a description of the allegations and the documents the claimant (or his attorney) presented to you.

Attorney Selection

Recalling my comments earlier in this book, each insurer has his own policy terms and conditions. The issue of selecting an attorney to assist in a claim is no different.

Under most bank directors' and officers' insurance, you will select your own attorney with your insurer's approval. Some policies will have a list of approved attorneys. You usually are still able to submit your own attorney for use.

Claim Settlement

Most policies do not allow the insured to settle claims without the approval of the insurance company. The result of such action is a claim that the insurance company won't pay.

It seems to happen often in the banking world. A customer is "injured" by some action taken by the bank—loan turned down, improper allocation of funds to an account, an embarrassing check refusal—and the bank president decides to "do the right thing." While such action may be ethically correct, it also may jeopardize coverage under the bank's insurance.

Most insurer D&O claims staff are professionals. Due to the complexities of these claims, many of the adjusters are attorneys. Most of them welcome calls from an insured (and consultants, fortunately).

Take a moment and talk with your insurer before you offer a settlement—even on a small claim.

Chapter Thirty-One: Fraud Bond Claims Help

The financial institutions bond responds to a wide range of fraud losses discovered during the policy period. The bank usually has sixty days from discovery of the event to report the loss to the insurance company.

Under most policies, if a claim is greater than 50 percent of the deductible amount, the claim must be reported to the insurer.

You have six months from discovery to file a proof of loss with your insurer.

I normally recommend bringing your insurer into bond claims quickly. While you may be experiencing a specific type of claim for the first time, your insurer has dealt with such issues hundreds of times. The claims department of your insurance company can save you many hours and a great deal of frustration. The department can also help you "plug the leaks" so that further losses are minimized.

Chapter Thirty-Two: Loss Control Ideas

Controlling losses and minimizing the impact of losses usually equals money well spent. Here are some general hints.

Property Loss Control

All locations should have walk-through inspections at least twice a year. Look for fire hazards such as the use of extension cords, broken or uncovered electrical outlets, paper materials near break room stoves, and accumulation of boxes or trash in storage areas. Are fire extinguishers up-to-date?

Document the property you own. Have someone take pictures of the inside and outside of your offices and branch locations. Videos can work well too. Store the photos (or the digital images) away from your location. Make two copies. Store one in the main office and another in a branch location.

Review fire extinguisher use with all employees at least once a year. Branch managers can use ten minutes in a staff meeting to go over proper use of the extinguishers at their location. No special training is needed for the trainer—read the instructions on the extinguisher. (OSHA wants you to do this too.)

Regularly review evacuation procedures with all employees at all locations. Test alarms at least every three months.

Inspect all locations at night, looking for adequate lighting of parking areas and around the building. Proper lighting discourages vandalism.

Consider installing video cameras in parking areas and locations susceptible to vandalism. Cameras help with slip and fall allegations, too.

Are overhang and awning heights clearly marked? Consider installing warning barriers that will alert drivers before their too-tall vehicles hit the building.

Are all the parking areas adjacent to your buildings equipped with parking guards to prevent vehicles from rolling into the side of the building?

Are ATMs and other drive-up areas properly guarded against damage caused by vehicles coming too close?

Liability Loss Control

Insist on clear walkways and sidewalks during winter storms.

Use nonslip surfaces in entryways and corridors. Assign an employee at each location with the responsibility of keeping areas dry that are otherwise prone to tracked-in water during rainstorms.

Remind branch personnel of the importance of responding quickly to slippery and hazardous conditions. (I've seen far too many reports of slip and fall accidents that begin with the phrase, "Several people had slipped in the entryway during the morning. ..." If only someone had put out a nonslip mat after the first person slipped!)

Tiled restroom floors should be regularly treated to retain their nonslip characteristics.

Instruct all branch managers on the proper procedure for handling slip and fall claims.

Have a disposable camera available at all locations to document the conditions at the time of a reported injury.

Be aware of food safety issues when snacks are put out for customers.

Workers' Compensation Loss Control

Preventing claims is the best approach to controlling your workers' compensation costs. No claims means low premiums.

What services does your insurance company offer that can help you with this? Many insurers have training programs and training tapes for your use.

Have an active safety committee with the authority to impact operations. No showcase committees—demand real, engaged, pragmatic work by a group of interested employees.

Have regular walk-through inspections looking for hazards.

Review the circumstances and facts of all incidents. Learn from past mistakes. What could have been done to prevent the problem?

Lead by example. If your company's policy requires stretch breaks, then management needs to participate too—be out there with everyone else. Employees watch the boss and follow his or her example.

Make some aspect of safety a part of every employee meeting. It can be a review of fire extinguisher use or a discussion on the importance of having ergonomically correct workstations. There is a natural way to include safety in all aspects of the operation. Safety is a habit.

Place emergency phone number stickers on the phones. Include emergency and nonemergency numbers for the police and fire departments. Don't forget about poison control as well. The national hotline of the American Association of Poison Control Centers is 1-800-222-1222. All these numbers are available in the front of most phone books.

Consider ergonomic issues when designing work areas. What can be done to lessen strain and repetitive motion issues? How can lifting exposures be engineered to reduce claims?

Appendix One: Insurance Terms

Accident: An event or occurrence that is unforeseen and unintended.

Actual Cash Value: Property insurance valuation method. The replacement cost of property damaged or destroyed at the time of loss, less depreciation.

ACV: Actual Cash Value

ADA: Americans with Disabilities Act

Additional Insured: A person or organization that meets the definition of an insured within an insurance policy. The party is not named specifically, but it is insured due to a group or class (e.g., employees, officers, and directors).

Additional Named Insured: A person or organization, other than the first named insured, specifically named as an insured in the declarations of the policy.

Adjuster/Adjustor: A person who investigates and settles losses for an insurance company. May be an employee of the insurer or an employee of an independent adjusting firm.

Advertising Injury: Injury arising out of an offense committed in the course of advertising activities. Examples include libel, slander, defamation, violation of right of privacy, piracy, unfair competition, or infringement of copyright, title, or slogan.

Agent: A legal representative of an insurance company. The agent's role in the insurance transaction is to sell and service insurance. This person may be an employee. See also Independent Agent, Direct Writer, and Captive Agent.

Agent of Record: See Broker of Record

Aggregate Limit: A limitation in many liability policies stipulating the maximum amount available for the total of all claims paid in a period of time. Aggregates are usually annual.

Agreed Amount Endorsement: An endorsement to property insurance policies that removes the penalty for coinsurance issues by agreeing that the amount of insurance meets any coinsurance requirements.

All Risk: Antiquated term to describe the perils in a property insurance policy. It has been replaced by the term "special risk." Using "all" got insurers and agents into trouble. See Special Risk.

Application: A form completed by the insured and/or the agent, providing information used in the underwriting and pricing process. The application becomes a part of the insurance policy for many lines of insurance.

ARAP: Rating system for assigned risk insurance programs managed by some states.

ARP: Assigned Risk Plan

Assessable Policy: An insurance policy that allows insurers to return to policyholders (as a group) for additional funds to cover losses of the group greater than anticipated. Usually only utilized in mutual insurance companies and captive/self-insurance plans.

Assigned Risk Plan: Also known as "The Pool." This is a risk-sharing mechanism set up by states to provide insurance for employers where no standard insurance company is interested. The problem may be with the risk (poor loss experience) or with the state's workers' compensation system (the state insurance has set up a system where insurers feel that they cannot make money).

Associate in Risk Management (ARM): Professional designation. A course of study including the management of risks using techniques other than insurance.

Audit Worksheet: The document prepared by the auditor that outlines the payrolls of your company. In many cases, the worksheet will show the remuneration of each employee and the classification assigned to that individual. The information on the worksheet is used to calculate the final premium.

Audited Premium: The final premium based upon the audited, actual payrolls.

Auditor: See Premium Auditor.

Average Weekly Wage: A wage figure used to determine the payout in lost wages to an employee injured in a workers' compensation loss.

B&M: See Boiler & Machinery Policy.

Bailee: An individual or entity that holds property of another. Examples are dry cleaners, jewelers, appliance repair firms, and computer repair firms.

Bailee Insurance: Insurance on the property of others held by a bailee.

Banker's Blanket Bond: See Financial Institutions Bond.

Banker's Professional Liability Insurance: Coverage for wrongful acts by the bank in the relationship with a customer. Usually a section of the directors' and officers' insurance.

BI: Bodily Injury

BII: Business Income Insurance or Business Interruption Insurance.

Binder: An oral or written statement that insurance coverage has been placed in effect. Usually issued by an insurance agent or the insurance company pending the actual policy being issued.

Blanket Insurance: A single limit of property insurance that insures multiple classes of property (buildings and contents) over multiple locations. Specific insurance provides specific coverage to a specific property. Blanket coverage lumps all property into one amount of insurance.

Bodily Injury: Injury or death. Some liability policies include emotional distress in the definition.

Boiler & Machinery Policy: Provides coverage for damage to equipment and machinery by mechanical breakdown, power surge, etc.

BOP: Business Owners' Policy

BOR: See Broker of Record.

BPL: Banker's Professional Liability

Broker: An insurance professional who represents the insured in the insurance transaction. Sometimes used incorrectly as a synonym for agent.

Broker of Record Letter: A form letter used to indicate a policyholder's preference to an insurance company as to which insurance agent will have exclusive rights to the insured. Excludes all other agents/brokers from accessing the insurance company in question for that policyholder.

Builder's Risk Insurance: Property insurance designed to protect buildings under construction or renovation. The policy recognizes the unique issues and hazards of construction. The rating of the policy recognizes the increasing values at risk.

Burglary: Breaking and entering into another person's building with felonious intent.

Business Income Insurance: See Loss of Business Income.

Business Insurance: A subset of insurance that applies to the risks and hazards of business ventures, as opposed to personal insurance.

Business Interruption Insurance: Part of property insurance that pays for the lost profits and continuing expenses that result from physical damage to insured property caused by an insured peril. See also Loss of Business Income, Extra Expense.

Business Owner's Policy: A package of insurance coverage providing both property and general liability insurance. Usually designed for smaller retail and office businesses.

Cafeteria Plan: See Flexible Benefit Plan.

Cancellation: Discontinuance of an insurance policy prior to policy expiration. May be at the request of the insured or by the insured's action (nonpayment of premium). In extreme cases, the insurance company cancels a policy for an increase in hazard. Cancellations are largely governed by state law.

Captive Agent: An insurance agent who represents a single insurer or a single group of insurers. Captive agents may have to give their represented insurers first right of refusal, or may be barred from accessing other insurers altogether.

Captive Insurance Company: An insurance company, owned by one or more noninsurance companies, formed to provide insurance coverage for the owners.

Carrier: The insurance company.

Casualty Insurance: Classification of insurance dealing with losses caused by issues of liability through bodily injury, personal injury, wrongful acts, or property damage. This includes:– auto insurance– general liability– workers' compensation– professional liability– directors' and officers' liability– fiduciary liability

Many casualty insurers also write surety business.

Cede: To transfer all or part of a risk written by an insurer to a reinsurer.

Certificate of Insurance: Proof of the existence at a moment in time of an insurance policy. Usually prepared by an insurance agent, it lists the coverage included in a program of insurance. Prepared for the information of a business associate of the insured—a subcontractor would have his agent issue a certificate to the general contractor.

Certified Insurance Counselor: Professional designation in property and liability insurance administered by the Society of Certified Insurance Counselors.

CGL: Commercial General Liability

CGL Policy: See Commercial General Liability Policy.

Chartered Property and Casualty Underwriter: Professional designation administered by the American Institute for Property and Liability Underwriters. The course of study includes extensive examinations covering the breadth of property and casualty insurance issues.

CIC: See Certified Insurance Counselor.

Claims Made: Refers to the trigger of liability coverage. An occurrence policy responds to events that happen (occur) during the policy period. Claims-made policies respond to lawsuits filed (the making of a claim) during the policy period.

Classification: Work comp. See Employment Classification.

Closed Claim: A claim that has been resolved. No further payments or treatments are expected.

CNP: Closed No Payment. Used on loss runs and claim reports to indicate that no payment was made on a claim, and the file has been closed.

Coinsurance: A penalty clause in property insurance policies that requires a certain percentage of the property's value to be insured. For example: A building with a replacement cost of $1 million and an 80 percent coinsurance clause must be insured for at least $800K (80 percent of the $1 million value) or a penalty is assessed at the time of a loss. Coinsurance in health insurance means the percentage of a loss paid by the insurance company. Liability insurance policies may have a coinsurance clause that denotes the percentage of the loss paid by the insurance company.

Collision Insurance: Auto Insurance—coverage for damage caused to the insured vehicle by an automobile accident or upset of the vehicle. Damage caused by collision with an animal or bird is covered by comprehensive automobile insurance.

Combination Safe Depository Policy: Covers losses to customers' property in a safe depository due to a loss or damage from actual or attempted burglary or robbery. Policies may exclude cash and coins.

Commercial Auto Policy: Provides protection for liability arising out of the use of motor vehicles. Also provides physical damage coverage to specified vehicles (also known as comprehensive and collision coverage).

Commercial Crime Insurance: Coverage forms used to insure against burglary, robbery, or counterfeit currency for organizations other than banks and financial institutions.

Commercial Crime Policy: Crime insurance used by general businesses. Banks use the financial institutions bond.

Commercial General Liability Policy: Provides coverage for bodily injury and property damage either from operations or products.

Commercial Lines Insurance: A broad category of insurance indicating coverage for businesses, professionals, and commercial establishments.

Commercial Property Policy: Coverage for buildings and contents.

Computer Coverage Property insurance covering computer hardware, software, and data. Considered inland marine insurance.

Conditions: Qualifications on the terms made by an insurance company—insured must pay premiums, insured must notify insurance company of claims, etc.

Consolidated Omnibus Budget Reconciliation Act (COBRA): Health insurance. A federal law that provides certain former employees, retirees, spouses, and dependent children the right to temporary continuation of health coverage at group rates. Coverage is limited to eighteen months.

Coverage: The scope of protection of an insurance policy. Used as a synonym for insurance.

CPCU: See Chartered Property and Casualty Underwriter.

Credit Insurance: Coverage against default by creditors. Insureds can protect all of their accounts receivable or specific creditors. Some credit insurance companies also provide credit watch and account receivable advisory services.

CSR: See Customer Service Representative.

Customer Service Representative: An employee of an insurance agency or company that provides administrative and customer support functions.

Cyber Liability Insurance: See E-Banking Insurance

D&O: Directors' and Officers' Insurance

Death Benefit: Payment made to a policy beneficiary upon death.

Debit Card Coverage: Can be included in the financial institutions bond. Provides coverage for loss resulting directly from the fraudulent use of a debit card to obtain cash or pay for products or services by gaining access to an electronic payment device, provided that such device, as part of the transaction, electronically verifies the customer's available funds in the customer's depository account at the insured's bank.

Debris Removal Clause: Extends property insurance to include payment for the removal of the debris from an insured loss. Includes demolition, transportation, and disposal of the rubble.

Dec: Declarations page. See Declarations.

Declarations: The part of an insurance policy that specifically describes the limits, premiums, rates, names, and other information relative to a specific insured.

Deductible: The part of a claim paid for by the insured. A $5K property deductible means that the insured pays the first $5K of any fire damage or other insured loss.

Difference in Conditions Policy: A property insurance policy that provides additional perils such as earthquake and flood coverage.

Definitions: The part of an insurance policy that defines many of the words used in the policy. Most policies highlight terms that are defined or place the term in quotation marks to indicate that the word is defined in the policy.

Depository Bond: Bond (surety) to guarantee the safety of funds made by depositors and their availability for withdrawal as indicated in the terms of deposit. Generally used for municipalities and school districts.

DIC: Difference in Conditions policy

Direct Writer: An insurance company that does not work through independent insurance agents. Agents for direct writers are usually employees of the insurance company or in exclusive relationships with the insurance carrier. Liberty Mutual, State Farm, and Allstate are direct writers.

Directors' & Officers' Insurance Policy: Provides coverage for allegations of third parties for mismanagement, failure to act properly, and other "wrongful acts" against directors and officers. Coverage also can be included for the bank, known as Entity Coverage

Discovery Period: See Extended Reporting Period.

Dishonesty Insurance: See Commercial Crime Policy.

Dividend: A return of premium given after a policy has expired based on loss experience of the insured or of a group of insureds. Low losses result in higher dividends. Under most state laws, insurers cannot guarantee dividends.

DOC: See Drive Other Car coverage.

Domestic: See Residence Employee.

Domestic Insurer: An insurer domiciled in a state in which the insured's insurance is written.

Drive Other Car Coverage: An endorsement to the commercial auto policy that extends coverage for individuals who are provided personal use of a company vehicle and are not covered by a personal auto policy.

Earned Premium: Premium used in an insurance policy. In workers' compensation, premium is earned as the employer incurs payroll expense.

E-Banking Insurance: Insurance designed to provide coverage for certain exposures unique to banking conducted over the Internet. Generally includes coverage for computer privacy liability, business interruption, copyright infringement, and public relations expense.

E-Commerce Insurance: See E-Banking.

EDP: Electronic Data Processing

EE: Extra Expense

EL: Employers' Liability

Employee Retirement Income Security Act: US federal law passed in 1974 that provides regulation over employee welfare plans—retirement funds, group insurance, pensions, etc.

Employers' Liability: The second part of workers' compensation insurance policies. Provides protection from liabilities that arise out of the employment relationship but are not covered by workers' compensation. For example: a spouse of an employee who becomes ill because of chemical residues brought home on the employee's clothing.

Employment Classification: The job code/description used to categorize employees and exposures.

Employment Practices Liability Insurance (EPLI): Liability insurance for acts of harassment, wrongful discharge, wrongful hiring, and discrimination.

Endorsement: Additional policy coverage, conditions, or exclusions added to the insurance contract by the insurance company. Sometimes called a Rider.

Entity Coverage: An extension of directors' and officers' insurance, providing coverage for legal actions against the insured entity.

EPLI: Employment Practices Liability Insurance

ERISA: See Employment Retirement Income Security Act.

ERISA Bond: Provides the required protection for the assets of a retirement fund under the federal law known as ERISA

E-Risk Insurance: See E-Banking.

Errors and Omissions Insurance: See Professional Liability Insurance.

Estimated Premium: Premiums determined at the beginning of a policy period based upon estimated payrolls. The insured pays for the policy based upon the estimated premium, and then the audit determines the final premium.

Excess and Surplus Lines: See Surplus Lines.

Excess Liability Policy: See Umbrella Liability.

Excess Loss Premium Factor: A part of retrospective rating programs. A factor to compensate the insurer for limiting the effects of losses over a certain amount, $50K for example.

Excess Losses: Part of the experience modification calculation. The amount of a loss that exceeds $5K. See also Primary Losses.

Exclusion: A part of an insurance contract that removes coverage for a specific set of circumstances. Flood is excluded from coverage on most property insurance policies.

Exclusive Agent: See Captive Agent.

Experience Modification Factor: A premium adjustment factor based upon the losses of a risk compared to losses of similar organizations. A ratio of expected losses to actual losses. Calculated by rating bureaus such as NCCI.

Experience Period: Policy and claim periods used in the experience modification (mod), usually the oldest three of the past four years. The 2006 mod is based on the data from years 2004, 2003, and 2002.

Exposure: A vulnerability to loss.

Exposure Basis: A unit of measuring exposure. In workers' compensation, the exposure basis is remuneration. In the case of some rates for domestic help, the unit may be per employee. A liability policy may use payroll, sales, or area as the basis of premium.

Extended Discovery Period: See Extended Reporting Period.

Extended Reporting Period: A provision included in claims-made liability insurance policies where, after the expiration or cancellation of a policy, the insured can extend the time to discover a claim that occurred prior to the end of the policy. Also called a Tail or Discovery Period.

Extortion: Extracting money or forcing actions based on a threat of harm. A part of most kidnap and ransom insurance policies.

Extra Expense Insurance: A part of time element insurance that pays the increased costs necessary to get an insured back into business quickly after insured property is damaged by an insured peril.

Federal Employees' Compensation Act: Workers' compensation act for federal civilian government employees. Overseen by the government of the United States. Does not involve private insurers or state funds.

Federal Employers' Liability Act (FELA): Applies to railway workers who are exempt from workers' compensation statutes. Cases decided on the basis of employers' liability.

Fellow Servant Rule: Archaic term used as a common-law defense for employers prior to workers' compensation laws. Held that an employer was not liable for injuries to an employee if the injury was caused by a fellow employee.

Fidelity Bond: See Commercial Crime Policy.

Fiduciary: A person entrusted with property or the care of an asset.

Fiduciary Coverage: See Fiduciary Liability Insurance.

Fiduciary Duty: The duties expected of a fiduciary.

Fiduciary Liability Insurance: Protects the fiduciaries, directors, and officers of employee welfare plans (group insurance, pension plans, 401(k) plans) against actual or alleged wrongful acts. Covers liabilities imposed by the federal law ERISA.

Financial Institutions Bond: Pays for dishonest acts by employees or outsiders. Theft of money, forgery, counterfeit currency, damage by hackers, etc.

Fire Insurance: Broad term used to describe building and personal property insurance protection.

Fire Legal Liability: A part of the commercial general liability insurance policy that protects damage to the part of the building occupied by the insured that is damaged due to the insured's negligence. Usually called upon to protect tenants for damage to the portion of the building they rent.

First Named Insured: The first person or organization listed on an insurance policy as an insured. First named insureds receive all policy notices and bills.

Flexible Benefit Plan: An employee benefit plan that allows employees to select among the various group life, medical expense, disability, dental, and other plans that best meet their specific needs.

Flood Insurance: Insurance against the peril of a general and temporary increase in the level of a stream, lake, river, or ocean.

Forced-Placed Insurance: Property insurance designed to cover properties where the bank's customer (the mortgagee) has failed to buy his own property insurance. Usually written on a monthly reporting basis.

Foreign Insurer: An insurer domiciled in a state other than the one in which the insured's insurance is written.

Form: The contract of insurance that outlines terms and conditions of protection.

FRIP: Fiduciary Responsibility Insurance Policy

Garagekeeper's Insurance: Provides coverage for the liability of parking vehicles owned by others.

General Liability: See Commercial General Liability.

GL: General Liability

Governing Classification: The employment class with the highest remuneration on a policy, except for standard exception classifications.

Group Self-Insurance: Many employers banding together to insure their operations based on a pooling of exposures and risks. They become an insurer. Groups can be homogeneous (a bank workers' compensation group) or heterogeneous (a plumber, a lumber yard, and a bank band together).

Guaranteed Cost: A workers' compensation program that is not subject to adjustments in premiums based on losses. Guaranteed cost programs include audits, and premiums are adjusted based on changes to remuneration.

Hammer Clause: A provision in a professional liability policy or directors' and officers' insurance that limits the insurer's liability should the insured refuse to accept a settlement offer from the plaintiff.

Hard Market: A description of the insurance marketplace used to indicate a period of increasing rates and constricting coverage/availability. A sellers' market. The opposite of a soft market.

Hazard: A situation that presents a chance of loss or an increase in the severity of a potential loss.

Incurred Losses: The total of amounts paid and amounts reserved.

Indemnification: An agreement where one party agrees to provide protection for certain legal actions brought against the primary party by another.

Indemnity: As to property insurance—a legal principle that holds an insured should not collect more than what he or she lost in a claim. As to work comp— lost time payments, as opposed to medical bills.

Indemnity Contract: As to liability—a provision that the insurance company reimburses an insured after settlement of a claim.

Independent Adjuster: A contractor of the insurance company who manages insurance claims for the insurance company.

Independent Agent: An autonomous business that sells and services insurance policies as a representative of a variety of insurance companies.

Inland Marine Insurance: A class of insurance covering articles in transit as well as the modes of transportation. Includes cargo, equipment, bridges, tunnels, art, jewelry, property owned by others, and other items.

Insurance: A contractual agreement where an insurance company assumes the risks outlined in an insurance policy in return for payment of a premium.

Insurance Adjuster: The person who manages the claim process for the insurance company. May be an employee of the insurer or a contractor hired by the insurer.

Insurance Carrier: See Insurance Company.

Insurance Commissioner: The top insurance regulatory official in a state. May be called a Superintendent.

Insurance Company: A commercial enterprise formed to sell and service insurance policies.

Interstate Rating: An experience modification that includes payroll and loss information from more than one state. Some states do not participate in interstate rating plans.

IRA-Keogh Errors & Omissions Policy: Covers errors in the administration of IRA and Keogh plans.

K&R: Kidnapping and Ransom Insurance. See Kidnap, Ransom, and Extortion Insurance

Kidnap, Ransom, and Extortion Insurance: Pays moneys demanded either for kidnapping or the threat of kidnapping. Also pays for extortion with a threat to property.

Liability: A legally enforceable obligation usually due to a breach of some duty or negligence.

Liability Insurance: Insurance that responds to a breach or negligence of the insured to another party.

Liquor Liability Insurance: Coverage designed to respond to liabilities arising out of the sale, manufacture, or serving of alcoholic beverages. Most commercial general liability policies exclude liquor liability claims only for those in the business of selling, manufacturing, or serving alcohol.

Longshoremen's and Harbor Workers' Act: See United States Longshoremen's & Harbor Workers' Act.

Loss: An accident or event that causes damage, injury, or illness.

Loss Adjustment Expenses: Monies spent to investigate and settle losses.

Loss Control: Practices and procedures used to minimize the severity of a loss. Also used to describe loss prevention activities.

Loss of Business Income: A part of time element insurance that pays for the lost profits and continuing expenses after damage to insured property caused by an insured peril.

Loss Prevention: Practices and procedures used to keep accidents from happening. Prevents frequency of loss. Also used to describe loss control activities.

Loss Ratio: Incurred losses (and loss adjustment expenses) divided by net premiums earned. Measures profitability. A measure of losses compared to premiums.

Loss Reserves: Estimated amounts for future payments of medical and wage payments for a specific claim.

Loss Run: A record of losses for a policy period.

Lost Wages: Amounts paid for wages lost by an employee due to a workers' compensation claim.

LTD: Long-Term Disability

Manual Premium: Calculated by multiplying payrolls by rate before application of any modification factors, schedule credits, or debits.

Manuscript Policy: A unique policy customized to the needs and exposures of a specific insured and a specific insurance company.

Medical Payments: General liability—coverage for medical bills incurred by a third party at an insured location. Coverage is not dependent on the negligence of the insured. Automobile—coverage for injuries to occupants of the insured vehicle caused by an auto accident.

Medical-Only Claims: Workers' compensation claims where there is no lost time/wages.

Misrepresentation: A false, incorrect, improper, or incomplete statement of a material fact made in the application for an insurance policy. Constitutes fraud in many states.

Mod: See Experience Modification.

Modified Premium: The workers' compensation premium after the application of the experience modification, but before other credits/debits are applied.

Monopolistic: A state workers' compensation system where no private insurers are allowed to compete for business.

MOP: Manufacturers' Output Policy.

Mortgage Errors and Omissions: Protects the bank's interest in properties mortgaged. Should a mortgage customer not purchase insurance (and the bank not know it), the policy will pay the bank's interest in the property should it be destroyed by a covered peril.

Mortgage Impairment Policy: See Mortgage Errors and Omissions

MP: Medical Payments

Mutual Insurance Companies: An insurance company owned by policyholders, as opposed to stockholders.

Named Insured: Individual(s) and organization(s) listed on the declarations as insured.

National Association of Insurance Commissioners (NAIC): Association of state insurance regulators who administer state insurance rules and laws. NAIC promotes uniformity in regulation throughout the country.

The National Council on Compensation Insurance (NCCI): The organization responsible in most states for administering classifications, experience modification factors, and collecting data used in rate-making. NCCI is not connected with any state government. It is a rate- and rule-making organization funded by insurance companies that use their services. They report information to states and are certainly regulated by state insurance departments. It is not, however, a government-run organization. They do act like it sometimes, though.

Net Premium: Premiums after all fees, charges, and credits.

NOC: As to work comp—see Not Otherwise Classified.

No-Fault Automobile Insurance: An approach used by certain states for liability issues resulting from auto accidents. Injuries resulting from auto accidents are paid for by the insurance covering the vehicle occupied by the injured person, rather than who was negligent.

Noncancelable: A policy feature that provides a guarantee of continuation of insurance at the insured's option. Insurers may adjust premiums, however.

Not Otherwise Classified: As to work comp—a term used in the Scopes® classification manual and other rule books to indicate employment classifications that are not included in other class descriptions.

Occupational Disease: An illness or disease resulting from a work hazard or condition.

Occupational Hazard: A condition in a job or work environment that increases the peril of accident, sickness, or death.

Occurrence: Defined by most liability policies as "an accident, including continuous or repeated exposure to substantially the same general harmful conditions."

Ocean Marine Insurance: Insures boats, vessels, and cargo transported over water.

OD: Occupational Disease.

Ordinance or Law Insurance: A part of property insurance that pays the increased cost of construction due to new zoning or building codes. Can also pay for demolition of the undamaged portion of a building that must be torn down due to violation of codes or ordinances. All coverage is triggered by a covered cause of loss plus the required action of laws or codes.

Other States: Work comp—the section of the policy that describes how coverage will apply outside of the states listed in the classification page of your policy.

Package Policy: Combining two or more insurance coverage sections into a single policy—property and liability coverages, for example. Homeowners' and business owners' policies are package policies.

Partial Disability: Work comp—impairment of a part of the body. May be permanent or temporary.

Payroll Audit: Work comp—an examination of employer records to determine final remuneration in individual employment classifications for the purpose of determining policy premium. Performed by an auditor.

Pending and Prior Litigation: An exclusion in many claims-made insurance policies for claims that were known prior to the inception date of the policy.

PD: Property Damage

Peril: A cause of loss—fire, lightning, hail, and robbery are examples of perils.

Permanent Partial Disability: Partial impairment of a part of the body that is not reversible and will not heal—amputation of a finger, for example. May not impair work capacity for certain occupations. May remove an employee from the current occupation.

Permanent Total Disability: Total loss of work capacity that is not reversible or will not heal.

Personal Injury: Usually a part of the commercial general liability insurance policy. Provides coverage for libel, slander, false arrest, or defamation of character. Actual definition varies by policy.

Personal Injury Liability Insurance: Part of the commercial general liability insurance policy that provides protection for libel, slander, defamation, or violation of right of privacy; and wrongful entry, eviction, or other invasion of right of private occupancy.

Personal Injury Protection (PIP): Auto insurance. See No-Fault.

Personal Lines: Insurance coverage in property and casualty insurance for families and households—personal auto coverage and homeowner's insurance, for example.

PI: Personal Injury

Policy: The insurance contract. It spells out the terms, conditions, and exclusions of the insurance provided by the insurance company.

Policy Term: The period of time that the insurance policy is in force.

Policyholder: The person or organization that owns the insurance policy.

Pollution: A cause of loss that is excluded by most property and liability insurance policies. Usually requires a special pollution liability insurance policy.

Pool: See Assigned Risk Plan.

Premium: The price of insurance for a specified risk for a specified period of time.

Premium Auditor: Work comp—an individual who performs the audit of remuneration at the end of a policy period. May be an employee of the insurance company or a contractor hired by the insurance company.

Premium Discount: Work comp—a premium credit based on the size of the premium paid.

Premium Finance: Finance arrangement for the insured to make payment of the insurance premium.

Primary Insurance: The insurance policy that is responsible for paying the first part of a loss. Excess policies pay after primary policies pay.

Primary Losses: Work comp—part of the experience modification calculation. The first $5K of any loss. See also Excess Losses.

Product Liability Insurance: Protection from legal actions against an insured for bodily injury and property damage caused by a product sold, manufactured, processed, or provided by the insured.

Professional Liability Insurance: Insurance against negligent damage caused by a wrongful act of the insured. Usually excludes bodily injury and property damage. Also called malpractice insurance. Also called errors and omissions insurance.

Proof of Loss: Presentation by the insured of documentation of the extent of a claim. Usually used in property insurance policies as a condition. Insurers must respond (pay) within a certain time to the presentation by the insured of a proof of loss.

Property Damage: Physical damage to tangible property.

Property Insurance: Insurance protection for loss of tangible property owned by or in the care of the insured. Includes buildings, personal property, stock, inventory, and time element insurance.

Property Policy: See Commercial Property Policy.

Protection and Indemnity Insurance: Specialized insurance for boats and commercial vessels. Responds to the unique exposures of maritime law and federal laws such as the Jones Act.

Public Adjuster: A person or firm that is a representative of the insured in a claim for insurance benefits.

Rating Bureau: Work comp—an organization that compiles statistical and rate-making information to determine premiums. See NCCI. Non-NCCI states have their own rating bureaus.

RC: Replacement Cost

Registered Mail Insurance: Provides insurance for loss, damage, or destruction of securities and other important or valuable papers during shipment.

Rehabilitation Benefits: Benefits payable to return an injured worker to work after a work-related injury or illness.

Reinsurance: Insurance purchased by insurance companies to provide a risk transfer mechanism. Also used by self-insurers and self-insured groups.

Remuneration: Payroll and other compensation paid to employees. Used to calculate premiums.

Renewal: The re-establishment of an insurance policy after the expiration of a prior term of coverage.

Replacement Cost: Property valuation method that uses the cost of replacement of an item or the cost of new construction without any deduction for depreciation.

Reservation of Rights: A response to a claim whereby the insurance company defends a case without any commitment as to the coverage provided by a policy.

Reserve: Amount expected to be paid on a claim that is not resolved or closed.

Residence Employee: Work comp—a person who performs full- or part-time household services.

Residual Market: See Assigned Risk Plan.

Retention: Amount of a claim paid by the insured. The term is usually used in liability insurance. Similar to a deductible.

Retention Plan: A loss-sensitive insurance plan that adjusts the premium up or down based on losses and associated costs.

Retrospective Rating: A loss-sensitive workers' compensation insurance program where adjustments are made to premiums after policy expiration. Adjustments can go up or down subject to premium minimums and maximums.

Rider: See Endorsement.

Risk: (1) Exposure to loss, (2) an insured, or (3) a portion of an insured operation.

Risk Management: The process of addressing, in a systematic way, the hazards and exposures of an organization. Risks can be avoided, reduced, transferred, and retained.

Insurance transfers the risk (or a part of it) to an insurance company.

Risk Retention Group: Alternative risk financing tool where similar businesses band together to share risks. Usually utilizes reinsurance and individual retentions along with regimented loss control and claims management process. Meets the requirements of the Risk Retention Act of 1986.

Safe Depository: See Combination Safe Depository.

Schedule Credit/Debit: Premium adjustment factors applied at the discretion of insurance company underwriters and based upon individual characteristics of the risk. Issues such as managed care, quality of management, loss control efforts, and the insurance company's appetite for the risk are included.

Scopes® Manual: Work comp—a publication of NCCI that outlines the definitions of the six hundred-plus employment classifications.

Second Injury Fund: Work comp—a mechanism set up by states to minimize the impact of re-injuries. The theory is that employers will be reluctant to hire previously injured workers without such a system. Sometimes funded by surcharges on insurers for death claims where there are low medical bills.

Self-Insurance: Retention of the risk usually in a formal, calculated way. In workers' compensation, state regulations impose financial and administrative qualifications. May involve reinsurance or very large deductibles to cover catastrophic losses. Self-insurance isn't really insurance—you are retaining the risk.

Self-Insured Retention: See Retention.

Short-Rate Penalty: A penalty assessed when an insurance policy is cancelled by the insured in the middle of a policy period. Workers' compensation short-rate penalties are high in the early months and gradually decline throughout the policy period. Short-rate penalties in other property and casualty policies are usually 10 percent of the unearned premium.

Side A: Coverage within a directors' and officers' insurance policy that pays for claims against individual directors or officers when corporate reimbursement isn't allowed.

Side B: Coverage within a directors' and officers' insurance policy that pays for claims against individual directors or officers when corporate reimbursement is allowed.

Side C: Coverage within a directors' and officers' insurance policy that pays for claims against the bank. Also referred to as entity coverage.

Sliding Scale Dividend: A dividend plan that varies the size of the dividend payment based on the loss ratio of the insured.

Soft Market: A description of the insurance marketplace used to indicate a period of declining rates and expanding coverage/availability. A buyers' market. The opposite of a hard market.

Sole Remedy: Workers' compensation is said to be the sole remedy for an employee's workplace injuries. In most states, employees may not seek payment from employers outside of workers' compensation for an employer's negligence or liability for an injury.

Special Risk: A type of property insurance policy where all perils (causes of loss) are insured except those that are excluded by the policy. Some common exclusions: flood, earthquake, animals, nuclear, and deterioration.

STAMP Bond: Securities Transfer Agents Medallion Program—provides signature guarantee.

Standard Exception Classifications: Work comp—employment classifications that are allowed on most policies in addition to the primary business classes.

Clerical, sales, and driver are common standard exceptions.

Standard Markets: Insurance companies that are not surplus lines insurers.

Standard Policy: An insurance policy used by a preponderance of insurance companies to cover similar exposures and operations.

Standard Premium: Work comp—premium after application of the experience modifier and schedule credits or debits, but before premium discount.

State Fund: A workers' compensation insurance system run by a state governmental agency. May be competitive with private insurers, or monopolistic. Also synonymous with assigned risk fund or pool.

STD: Short-Term Disability

Strict Liability: Liability that comes out of an exposure that is so onerous that negligence need not be proven (e.g., blasting within a city, the keeping of wild animals).

Subrogation: The procedure under which an insurance company recoups losses paid from the insurer of the negligent or responsible party. For example, a workers' compensation insurer may subrogate against the auto insurer of the driver who caused an accident in which an employee is injured.

Surety Bond: An agreement that guarantees that the principal will fulfill its obligations to the obligee. Surety—bonding company. Principal—party performing the work. Obligee—entity for whom the principal is working to whom the surety is obligated.

Surplus Lines: Insurance written by non-admitted insurance companies.

Tail Coverage: See Extended Reporting Period.

Temporary Partial Disability: A condition where an injured worker's capacity is impaired for a time, but he or she is able to continue working at reduced capacity. Full recovery is expected.

Temporary Total Disability: A condition where an injured worker is unable to work at all while he or she is recovering from injury. Full recovery is expected.

Terrorism Risk Insurance Act: Federal law outlining the taxpayer-funded reinsurance provided for certain types of terrorism losses.

Time Element Insurance: A subset of property insurance that pays the lost profits, continuing expenses, and increased expenses caused by an insured peril. Usually triggered by damage to insured property. See Loss of Business Income. See Extra Expense Insurance.

Tort: A civil wrong other than a breach of contract.

TRIA: Terrorism Risk Insurance Act.

Trust Department Errors & Omissions Policy: Provides protection for claims made against a bank for losses resulting from an error or omission by the trust department while performing trust functions.

Twisting: Inaccurate or incomplete insurance policy descriptions used to entice the surrender or cancellation of an insurance policy in favor of another policy.

U&O: Use and Occupancy (antiquated term).

UIM: Under-Insured Motorist.

UM: Uninsured Motorist.

Umbrella Liability: A form of excess insurance that provides additional limits of liability protection as well as increasing the breadth of the coverage provided.

Umbrella Liability Policy: Provides extra liability coverage above the general liability, auto liability, and employers' liability coverage. Also known as excess liability.

Underlying Policies: The basic liability insurance policies that are accessed before excess or umbrella liability policies. Usually include auto liability, general liability, and employer's liability.

Underwriter: (1) An insurance company, or (2) the individual who performs underwriting for an insurance company.

Underwriting: The process an insurance company goes through to classify, analyze, and price an insurance policy.

Unearned Premium: The difference between the premium paid and the earned premium.

Uninsured/Underinsured Motorist Coverage: Autopays the policyholder for injuries to occupants of the insured vehicle if the accident was caused by a driver who has too little or no liability insurance.

Unit Stat Card: Work comp—a form filed with a rating bureau by an insurance company to report remuneration and losses on a specific policy. Used to calculate the experience modification. Usually submitted based on losses shown at the six-month point in a policy.

United States Longshoremen's & Harbor Workers' Compensation Act: Federal workers' compensation law that stipulates compensation for those who work in harbors and on wharves.

U.S.L. & H. See United States Longshoremen's and Harbor Workers' Compensation Act.

Voluntary Compensation: An endorsement to the standard workers' compensation insurance policy; extends coverage to employees not required to be covered under the state's workers' compensation law. Farm workers, domestic help, business owners, for example. Usually has nothing to do with volunteers. The term refers to the voluntary addition of normally uncovered individuals.

Voluntary Market: The standard insurance market where insurers offer coverage on a competitive basis. Assigned risk insurance programs (auto or workers' compensation) are involuntary markets. Also, insurance written outside of any assigned risk plan.

WC: Workers' Compensation

Workers' Compensation: (1) A state-mandated program of benefits for injured workers, and(2) an insurance policy designed to provide benefits based on a state's workers' compensation law.

Workers' Compensation Insurance: Pays benefits as provided by state law for work-related injuries or diseases. The policy also provides protection for other types of work-related incidents.

Appendix Two: Agent Selection Questionnaire

Note: You may submit this information in any format you wish as long as the information provided is complete. You do not need to use this form.

General Information About Your Firm

Your Firm's Name:

Mailing Address:

Physical Location:

Telephone   Fax:

Name of Contact Person: Email:

How many bank clients does your organization currently serve?

What is your approximate premium volume of bank business?

Account Management Team

Please attach a brief résumé for each person who would be handling our account. As a minimum, please be sure the following information is included:

Name and position	Length of time in insurance business
Licenses held	Length of time in your employment
Insurance work experience	Insurance designations earned
Specific experience with banks	Specific skills or expertise
Expected role on this account	

Please describe any specialized services that your firm has to offer, and that you feel would enhance your position in our evaluation.

References

List at least three bank clients or clients who have similar exposures.

Name:

Contact Name:

Phone:

Name:

Contact Name:

Phone:

Name:

Contact Name:

Phone:

Any reference you provide may be contacted without notice to you.

Market Allocation

You may not approach an insurer or reinsurer until given permission to do so by us. Failure to comply with this restriction may automatically disqualify you.

List in the order of your preference the insurers you wish to utilize in the bid process.

First Selection – Insurer Name:

Lines of Coverage:

Why are you the best agency to approach this insurer?

Second Selection – Insurer Name:

Lines of Coverage:

Why are you the best agency to approach this insurer?

Third Selection – Insurer Name:

Lines of Coverage:

Why are you the best agency to approach this insurer?

Use additional sheets as needed. You may submit as many insurers as you wish.

Miscellaneous Information

Feel free to add any additional information you feel would be useful in our evaluation.

Prequalification Questionnaire Authorization

This prequalification questionnaire is submitted with my approval, and is true and factual.

_____ Date:

Signature

Name:

Title: Organization:

Please return this form to:

<<NAME & ADDRESS>>

Appendix Three: Bid Summary Matrix

Here is a list of issues to consider when reviewing your current insurance or comparing proposals from several insurers. I like to use a matrix with the issues below in the first column. Use the subsequent columns for the other insurers.

Go to www.ScottSimmonds.com/bankbook for a free copy of this list in Microsoft Word format to make your job easier.

	Insurer A	Insurer B	Insurer C
Property Insurance			
Is Coverage Blanket or Specific?			
Blanket Building & Personal Property Limit			
Agreed Amount?			
Coinsurance?			

Special Perils?			
Property Valuation			
Flood Coverage			
Flood Limitations			
Flood Deductible			
Earthquake Coverage			
Earthquake Deductible			
Property Deductible			
Windstorm Deductible			
Debris Removal			
Building Ordinance			
Improvements and Betterments			
Personal Property of Others			
Personal Property Off-Premises			
Off-Premises Services			
Boiler & Machinery			
Accounts Receivable			
Computer Equipment			
Business Interruption			
Business Income			
Extra Expense			
Coinsurance			
Blanket All Locations?			

Agreed Amount			
Maximum Period of Indemnity			
Peril of Service Interruption			
Loss of Rental Income			
Casualty			
Occurrence CGL Form			
Occurrence Limit			
Aggregate Limit			
Fire Legal Limit			
Per Location Aggregate			
Premium Basis			
Auto Limit of Liability			
Non-Owned Auto Coverage?			
Drive Other Car Coverage			
Employees as Insured on Auto Policy			
Common Insurer for GL/Auto			
Owned Watercraft or Aircraft			
Pollution/Environmental Liability			
Workers' Compensation States			

Employers' Liability Limits			
Umbrella Limits			
Financial Institutions Fraud-Bond			
Fidelity			
On Premises			
In Transit			
Forgery and Alteration			
Securities Forgery			
Check Kiting			
Claims Expense			
Audit Expense Rider			
Computer Systems Coverage – Fraud			
Counterfeit Check			
Counterfeit Currency			
Destruction by Hacker			
Destruction by Virus			
Extortion			
Fraudulent Mortgage			
Injury/Death Indemnity			
Lost Instrument Bond			

Trading Loss			
Transit Cash Letter			
Unattended ATM			
Unauthorized Signature			
Fax Wire Fraud			
Telephone Wire Fraud			
Management Liability			
Directors' and Officers'			
Policy Limit			
Entity Coverage Included in Policy Limit			
Brokerage/Advisory Services			
Employment Practices Liability			
Trust E&O			
Insurance Agent E&O			
Coverage Trigger			
Lender Liability Limit			
IRA/Keogh			
Fiduciary			
Discovery Premium			
Employment Practices			
EPL Definitions			

Are Above Limits Separate Limits or Do They Deplete The Aggregate?			
Premiums			
Property			
Inland Marine			
Machinery Breakdown			
Liability			
Crime			
Auto			
Workers' Comp			
Umbrella			
Financial Institution Bond			
Safe Depository			
Directors and Officers			
Employment Practices			
Fiduciary			
Internet Liability			
Mortgage Impairment			
STAMP Bond			
Forced-Placed Property			
Lenders Single Interest			
Service Fees?			
Agency Service Expectations			
Frequency of Account Review			

Claims Department			
Producer Involvement in Account?			
Extent of Loss Control Services			
Phone/Email Return Policy?			
Insurer Issues of Concern			

Scott Simmonds, CPCU, ARM
Insurance Assurance Consulting
Phone: 207-284-0085
www.ScottSimmonds.com
20 Sofia Road, Saco, Maine 04072-9017

Consulting On, But Never Selling, Insurance

Bibliography

Bank Insurance and Risk Management, Standard Publishing Corporation, Boston, MA, www.spcpub.com, 1995 with quarterly updates. This is a publication I subscribed to for several years in the hope that it would provide insight and ideas. It did not. I am no longer a subscriber.

Burnham's Insurance Dictionary, Ray M. Burnham, II, Copyright 2009, www.BurnhamSystem.com This is an exceptional insurance reference work. I use it constantly.

About Me

I guess I was born to the insurance business. My dad was an insurance agent in New Hampshire when I was a baby. He then joined an insurance company, and we bounced about the East Coast while I was in school—Massachusetts, Ohio, Georgia, back to Massachusetts.

The summer between my freshman and sophomore year in college, I decided it was time to get a job in business. I thought I wanted to be a stockbroker. I rode into Boston every morning with my dad and would go from office building to office building, riding the elevator to the top floor and stopping at every office on each floor—moving down one elevator stop at a time asking if there was an opening for a college student.

After two weeks and no luck, my dad suggested I try an insurance agency. I got the job (as an auto claims clerk) and the rest has been thirty-plus years in the business—working at five different insurance agencies before starting my own consulting practice.

In 2000, I decided that there was a need for an insurance expert who did not sell insurance. I left my job at a small agency, and my wife allowed me to take over the corner of a basement bedroom.

As the business grew, my office grew from a corner, to half the bedroom, to taking over the family room. We then built a new house with a large office with a separate "office" entrance—a door that has not once been entered by a client.

That office now houses the largest solo-practitioner insurance consulting firm in the United States. I have clients in thirty-five states. I have been called the largest single insurance buyer in the country. Several years ago, I totaled it up—I help my clients with about $50 million in premium each year.

I graduated from Babson College in Wellesley, Massachusetts. In 1987, I earned the Certified Insurance Counselor designation from the Society of CIC. In 1995, I finished the work (ten essay exams given over five years) to qualify for the Chartered Property and Casualty Underwriter designation conferred by the American Institute for CPCU.

I earned the Insurance Institute of America's Associate in Risk Management designation in 2005. In 2007, I was awarded the Certified Management Consultant designation by the Institute of Management Consultants USA.

My insurance work has involved companies in a wide range of industries. I have handled insurance and risk management issues for public and private corporations, including many with international operations. My work includes nonprofits, manufacturers, banks, hotels, property managers, municipalities, and schools.

I hold a State of Maine resident insurance consultant's license and nonresident licenses in every state where I am required to do so—I think I'm up to twenty-eight state licenses now.

About ten years ago, I was accepted as a member of the Society for Advancement of Consulting, an organization made up of only the top 1 percent of consultants nationwide. Several years ago, I was granted "board approved" status, putting me in the top 10 percent of the top 1 percent of consultants.

My writing and comments have appeared in the *Wall Street Journal, Forbes, Fortune, Money, Inc. Magazine, Smart Money Magazine, The New York Times, Boston Globe, Investors Business Daily, Kiplinger's, The Los Angeles Times*, and countless trade publications.

I make my home in Saco, Maine. I enjoy the shooting sports, particularly competitive pistol shooting and trap. I also enjoy reading, playing with our dog, and bird watching. My wife and I have five kids and two grandchildren.

I'm a past president of the trade association, Maine Association Of Professional Consultants, and of the Biddeford Saco Rotary Club.

This second edition of Simmonds on Bank Insurance is my ninth insurance book.

For More Information Contact:
Scott Simmonds, CPCU, ARM
Unbiased "Fee-Only"Insurance Consultant
Email: Scott@ScottSimmonds.com
Web: www.ScottSimmonds.com
Phone: 207-284-0085

Questions or Comments?

I would love to hear your thoughts and ideas about this book. Email me at Scott@ScottSimmonds.com.

One Last Thing – If You Bought The Electronic Version

About 90 percent of the time, the site you bought this book from will add a page at the end of this book. They will give you an opportunity to rate the book and share your thoughts on Twitter and Facebook.

If you believe this book is worth sharing, would you take a few minutes to let your friends know about it?

Please also post your reactions to this book on my Amazon review page. Go to **http://goo.gl/QdPrw.**.

www.ingramcontent.com/pod-product-compliance
Lightning Source LLC
Chambersburg PA
CBHW071413170526
45165CB00001B/254